The International Federation of Library Associations and Institutions

A
GUIDE
TO CENTRES
OF
INTERNATIONAL
LENDING
AND
COPYING

4th EDITION
1990

Compiled and edited by

Margaret M Barwick

IFLA Office for International Lending
The British Library Document Supply Centre, Boston Spa, England

INTERNATIONAL FEDERATION OF LIBRARY ASSOCIATIONS AND INSTITUTIONS

FEDERATION INTERNATIONALE DES ASSOCIATIONS DE BIBLIOTHECAIRES ET BIBLIOTHEQUES

INTERNATIONALER VERBAND DER BIBLIOTHEKARISCHEN VEREINE UND INSTITUTIONEN

FEDERACION INTERNACIONAL DE ASOCIACIONES DE BIBLIOTECARIOS Y BIBLIOTECAS

Международная федерация библиотечных ассоциаций и учреждений

British Library Cataloguing in Publication Data

International Federation of Library Associations and Institutions

A guide to centres of international lending and copying. - 4th ed.

I.   National lending libraries. Directories
I.   Title
II. Barwick, Margaret M.
III. IFLA Office for International Lending
IV. International Federation of Library Associations and Institutions. Brief guide to centres of international lending and photocopying
027.5
ISBN 0-7123-2076-8

Distributed by:

The Publications Sales Unit
The British Library
Document Supply Centre
Boston Spa
Wetherby
West Yorkshire
LS23 7BQ
United Kingdom

Telephone: 0937 546077

Printed in the United Kingdom
by Hobbs the Printers of Southampton

CONTENTS

INTRODUCTION TO THE FOURTH EDITION

The first edition of A Brief Guide to Centres of International Lending and Photocopying was published in June 1975 and sold over 1,000 copies. Around 1,600 copies of the second edition, which was published in 1979, were sold. 1,990 copies of the third edition published in 1984 were sold. The Brief Guide has thus proved itself as a handy reference work for those actively involved in international lending. Continued demand for the third edition, together with the vital need for the information contained in the guide to be kept accurate and up-to-date, prompted the IFLA Office for International Lending to publish this, the fourth edition.

Information was again gathered by questionnaire, a copy of which is included in the Guide. Over 140 countries are included in this edition of the Guide, compared with 90 in the third edition. In some cases new information was not received and the entry from the third edition is therefore reproduced. Such countries are marked by an asterisk (*) in the text. Information in such entries may well be inaccurate, but is nevertheless included as the only information available.

In this fourth edition a new layout has been adopted removing the need to refer to a number code when consulting the country entries. A revised title has also been adopted to reflect the increase in the Guide's size and to take account of all means of copying. Copyright restrictions on copying have been assumed and are not therefore listed under each individual country.

It is generally accepted that many international requests for photocopies and microforms need not pass through the national centre and some additional institutions are listed for countries where this is possible. In accordance with International Lending: Principles and Guidelines for Procedure, revised in 1987, a copy of which is included in the Guide, additional institutions to which loan requests may be sent have also been included, where this information was supplied. For some countries (notably the USA) the number of these additional institutions would be so large that they have been omitted. Nevertheless, the generally smaller number of institutions per country appearing in this edition reflects the fact that IFLA recommendations on better organisation of interlending within countries have been acted upon in many cases. This is encouraging, as it greatly simplifies and streamlines both the requesting and supplying libraries' task.

The IFLA International Loan/Photocopy Request Form has now become widely used and many of the entries in this Guide specify a preference for requests to be made on this form. The form has recently been redesigned and a copy is reproduced in the Guide. Details of this form and supplies of it may be obtained from the IFLA Office for International Lending.

This edition of the Guide cannot pretend to be exhaustive. It must be emphasised that if international lending is to be carried out efficiently and with ease on the part of both requesting and supplying libraries, the published information presented must be as comprehensive, accurate and up-to-date as possible. Additions and corrections will therefore be welcomed.

Thanks are expressed to my colleagues, Paul Cleary, Alison Gallico, Stella Pilling and Richard Bennett for help in translating some of the questionnaires and for translating the lists of countries into the different languages. I am also most grateful to the typists, especially Pam Wainwright, who typed the majority of the Guide.

Correspondence concerning the Guide should be addressed to:

Margaret M Barwick
IFLA Office for International Lending
c/o British Library Document Supply Centre
Boston Spa
Wetherby
West Yorkshire
LS23 7BQ
United Kingdom

NOTES ON ARRANGEMENT OF ENTRIES

1. Countries are arranged alphabetically by their English name. Indexes to the countries are given in the five IFLA languages—English, French, German, Russian and Spanish.

2. Within each country entry different institutions may be grouped together if their policies are more or less consistent, or they may be dealt with separately if their policies differ widely.

3. Replies to individual questions are in some cases grouped together for clarity and to avoid unnecessary repetition of the same information.

4. In most cases the country is not given in the address of libraries in question 2. This is because this will differ according to the language of the requesting country. The name of the country should not, of course, be omitted when requests are sent out.

The entries in this 'Guide' were formulated on replies to the following questionnaire.

Country ....

BRIEF GUIDE TO CENTRES OF INTERNATIONAL LENDING AND COPYING—4TH EDITION

If your country does not have an interlending system, please return the questionnaire and explain this at Question 1.

1. Briefly describe the national and international lending system in operation: major lending collections and union catalogues: where to obtain copies of national guidelines (if any). If no interlending system exists, please state 'NO national system'. Please answer on a separate sheet of paper if necessary.

2. a. Centres to which LOAN requests should be sent. Include full postal address, telephone, telex, facsimile and electronic mail numbers. Give brief details of any special procedures when using telex, etc.

    b. Do the centres despatch material by air mail? If not, how is it despatched?

    c. Do the centres require that material be returned by air mail?

3. a. Centre to which request for PHOTODUPLICATED material should be sent with the same details as in 2a.

    b. Do these centres despatch material by air mail?

4. Any restrictions on certain categories of material for loan or photoduplication, other than copyright.

5. Type of request form preferred (for example IFLA forms) for international requests to your country.

6. Charges

    a. Loans. Do libraries charge for postal costs of individual items loaned? Are other charges made for loans?

    b. Photoduplicated material. What is the charge for copies per page or unit of pages?

    c. Charge for 35mm microfilm negative.

    d. Charges for 35mm positive.

    e. Paper copy.

    f. Duplicate microfiche.

    g. Paper copy from microfiche.

7. Method of payment or accounting used for:

    a. Loans.

    b. Photoduplicated material.

8. Period of loan.

9. Is renewal allowed? Under which circumstances?

10. Any other relevant information, for example, national libraries that do not participate in international lending/copying except as a last resort; whether material should be sent/returned through a national centre and any other relevant information to help those who might want a document from your country. Please use a separate sheet of paper if necessary.

Please remember to give the full name and address of the library completing this questionnaire.

INTERNATIONAL LENDING*: PRINCIPLES AND GUIDELINES FOR PROCEDURE (1978)—MAJOR REVISION 1987

The mutual use of individual collections is a necessary element of international cooperation by libraries. Just as no library can be self-sufficient in meeting all the information needs of its clientele, so no country can be self-sufficient. If the library service of a country is to be effective methods must be devised to obtain access to material held in other collections in other countries. International lending has as its aim the supply by one country to another, in the surest and fastest way, of documents that are not available in the country where they are needed.

The following guidelines, agreed by the Standing Committee of IFLA's Section on Interlending in 1978 and modified in 1987, represent a major revision of the Rules agreed by IFLA in 1954. While they have no mandatory force, and while every country must determine the ways in which it conducts interlending, the guidelines are strongly urged on individual countries and libraries as a basis for the conduct of international lending. They are preceded by a statement of Principles of international lending agreed in an earlier and slightly different version in 1976 by National Libraries and by the Standing Committee of IFLA's Section on Interlending, and are accompanied by a commentary which seeks to elucidate and amplify certain aspects of the guidelines.

PRINCIPLES OF INTERNATIONAL LENDING

1. Every country should accept responsibility for supplying to any other country, by loan or photocopy, copies of its own publications, certainly those published from the present date, and as far as possible retrospectively. This responsibility may be discharged in various ways, among which national loan/photocopy collections appear to have particular advantages.

2. Each country should have a national centre or centres to coordinate international lending activity for both incoming and outgoing requests. Such centres should be closely linked with, if not part of, the national library where there is one.

3. Each country should aim to develop an efficient national lending system, since national lending systems are the essential infrastructure of international lending.

4. As far as possible, photocopies or microfilms should be supplied in the place of loans of original copies.

5. Fast methods should be used for supplying and returning items. Airmail should be used whenever possible.

6. All requests should be dealt with expeditiously, having regard to accuracy, at all points: the requesting library, any intermediary used and the source library.

7. Standard and simple procedures should be developed and adopted, particularly procedures for requesting items and for reclaiming any payment.

---

*   'Lending' is held to include the sending of photographic and other reproductions in place of the original.

\#   This paper is also available in French, Spanish and Arabic.

GUIDELINES FOR PROCEDURE

1. **General**

   Each library should, within any nationally agreed policy, use the most efficient methods for identifying locations of wanted documents and transmitting requests.

   Commentary

   1.1 Speed of supply is extremely important to most users. Every effort should be made to follow routines which are simple and time-saving. International requests often take far longer to satisfy than those dealt with nationally so that procedures should be modified where necessary to reduce delays. All communications should be in clear and simple language and legible to avoid misunderstanding across linguistic barriers.

2. **National Centre for International Lending**

   2.1 Each country (or, in the case of federal countries, each state or province) should have a centre playing an active role in international lending. Its main functions are:

   a) to act as a centre for the receipt of requests from abroad and their transmission onward to libraries within its own country when direct access to collections is not possible or accepted;

   b) to act as a centre for the transmission of requests to foreign countries from libraries within its own country when direct access is not possible or not accepted;

   c) to provide where necessary bibliographical support and expertise to ensure that requests sent abroad reach the required standards;

   d) to gather statistical information from within its own country on international loan transactions and to send these figures regularly to the IFLA Office for International Lending.

   2.2 Centres for international lending may, and should where possible, also perform the following functions:

   a) to perform a coordinating role for national interlending;

   b) act as the main national centre for the supervision and construction of union catalogues and their maintenance;

   c) to have direct access to significant library collections in their own country;

   d) to provide an information service on interlending;

   e) to have responsibility for planning, developing and supervising an efficient national system of interlending where this function is not adequately performed by another agency.

   Commentary

   2. The nomination or establishment of national centres to carry out the functions mentioned in 2.1 and 2.2 is strongly recommended as the most efficient and effective means of carrying out these functions. In those countries where no such national centre has been nominated or established the following recommendations are made:

      2.1a Published guides, as comprehensive as possible, should be provided to facilitate the direction of requests by other countries. All libraries within the country should make strenuous efforts to observe the same procedures for handling and when necessary circulating requests received from other countries.

      2.1b In the case of loans of originals, individual libraries should accept responsibility for ensuring that no loanable copy of a required work exists in another library within the country before sending requests abroad. See 3.4 below.

      2.1c The collection of statistics, which is vital for monitoring trends and efficiency, should still be carried out on a national basis.

2.1d Strong coordination is essential if the international requirements and responsibilities of a country without a national centre are to be fulfilled efficiently. A coordinating body may be in a position to fulfil some of the functions of a national centre.

3. Procedure for Requesting

3.1 All requests using paper forms shall be on the forms authorized by IFLA, unless otherwise stipulated by the library to which requests are sent. Requests submitted by telex (TWX) or electronic mail shall conform to agreed standards.

3.2 To ensure that inadequate or inaccurate requests are not sent abroad the borrowing library shall verify, and where necessary complete, the bibliographic details of items requested to the best of its ability, giving the source of reference where possible. Where necessary or appropriate details shall be checked or completed by the national centre.

3.3 Requesting libraries should keep a record of all requests, each of which should have a serial number.

3.4 In the case of loans of originals, all reasonable efforts shall be made to ensure that no loanable copy is available in its own country before a request is sent abroad. Documents that are available in a country but are temporarily in use should only be requested on international loan in exceptional circumstance.

Commentary

3. <u>Requests for loans</u> should normally go through national centres, since otherwise it is very difficult to ensure that there is no other loanable copy in the country, and loans are expensive. It may be decided that it is easier, cheaper and faster to apply direct abroad (for example, when the only known location is outside the country); however, a record of all such requests should be sent to the national centre for information. <u>Requests for photocopies</u> may however in appropriate cases be made direct to foreign libraries, not necessarily in the country of publication.

3.1 Forms should wherever possible be completed in typescript.

3.2 Inadequate requests cause delays, and may have to be returned for further checking.

Where a request is inadequate because the requesting library has insufficient bibliographic resources to check it, it should be checked by the national centre or centres before it is despatched.

3.4 This is the responsibility of the appropriate national centre when no comprehensive record of national holdings is generally available.

3.5 Fast methods include airmail, telex, telefacsimile, direct computer transmission and electronic mail.

4. Procedure for Supplying

4.1 Every country has a special responsibility to supply its own national imprints on international loan. No country or library is under an obligation to supply a work that has been requested, but all reasonable efforts should be made to satisfy international requests.

4.2 Items shall be sent direct to the requesting library except where, for administrative reasons, it is specifically required that they should be sent to the national centre.

4.3 All documents lent should be clearly marked with the name of the owning library.

4.4 Packages containing items sent in response to requests shall be clearly marked: 'INTERNATIONAL LOANS BETWEEN LIBRARIES'.

4.5 No library receiving a request should normally retain it for longer than one week (two weeks in the case of difficult requests) before supplying the item or returning the request to the national centre or the requesting library.

4.6 When a request cannot be satisfied, the requesting library should be notified at once.

4.7 When the satisfaction of a request is likely to be seriously delayed, the requesting library should be notified at once.

Commentary

4.1 The responsibility of each country to supply its own national imprints is emphasized: without the acceptance of such a responsibility, both availability and speed of supply are seriously jeopardized. This responsibility is an essential element in Universal Availability of Publications.

4.4 Clear statements on the outside of packages are necessary to avoid problems with Customs.

4.5 Difficult requests include requests that require extensive bibliographic checking and requests that are satisfied by making copies of long documents (eg microfilms of books).

4.6 Failure to notify inability to supply or delays in supplying causes further delays and
& uncertainty in the requesting library. In countries with no national centre, fast procedures
4.7 should be devised to transmit to other libraries requests that cannot be satisfied. If such procedures are not possible, the requests should be returned at once to the requesting library.

5. Conditions of Supply

5.1 Where photocopies are supplied, libraries supplying and receiving them must abide by any requirements necessary to satisfy relevant copyright regulations.

5.2 Original documents when received by the borrowing library shall be used in accordance with its normal regulations, unless the supplying library stipulates certain conditions.

5.3 Items should be sent by the fastest postal service available.

Commentary

5.3 It is recognized that is some cases the use of airmail, although desirable, may not be possible because the cost cannot be borne by either the borrowing or the supplying library. The use of fast methods of transmission is nevertheless very strongly urged, since slower methods may make libraries reluctant to lend and inconvenience the individual user.

6. Period of Loan

6.1 The loan period, which shall in all cases be specifically and clearly stated, shall normally be one month, excluding the time required for despatch and return of the documents. The supplying library may extend or curtail this time limit.

6.2 Application for extension of the loan period shall be made in time to reach the supplying library before the loan period has expired.

7. Procedure for Returning

7.1 Documents lent should be returned by the fastest postal service available. Packages shall be marked 'INTERNATIONAL LOANS BETWEEN LIBRARIES'.

7.2 Libraries returning documents shall observe any special stipulations by supplying libraries with regard to packaging, registration etc.

7.3 Documents shall be returned to the supplying library except where return to the national centre is specifically stipulated.

7.2 Special stipulations may relate to special packaging in the case of fragile documents or registration in the case of rare items.

8. Receipts

No receipts shall be provided either for the supply of an item or its return to the supplying library, unless specifically requested.

9. Responsibility for Loss or Damage

From the moment a library despatches an item to a requesting library until it returns, the requesting library shall normally be responsible for any loss or damage incurred, and pay the supplying library the full estimated cost of such loss or damage, including where requested any administrative costs involved.

Commentary

It is in the interests of all concerned to ensure that all items are adequately packaged. Claims from supplying libraries for loss or damage cannot be seriously entertained if packaging by them has been inadequate.

Supplying libraries are expected to help where necessary with postal inquiries in cases of loss or damage.

10. Payment

Accounting and payment procedures should be minimized. Payment shall be made or waived according to agreements between the two countries or libraries involved. Payment between national centres or individual libraries receiving and providing a similar number of satisfied requests should be waived. Payment may also be waived when the number of items supplied to a particular country or library is so small as not to justify the accounting procedures involved.

Commentary

Simplified methods of payment include:

a) prepaid systems, whereby national centres or libraries buy numbers of coupons in advance, and send an appropriate number of coupons with each request;

b) deposit accounts, whereby the supplying library holds a sum deposited by a requesting library and deducts amounts from it according to each item supplied;

c) flat-rate payments, whereby average rather than individual costs are recovered; or unit payments, whereby charges are made in a limited number of units. Either of these methods may be combined with pre-payment or deposit accounts.

Payment may be made by national centres, which may recover it from requesting libraires in their countries, or direct by requesting libraries, according to the system in operation in the requesting country. The requirements of the supplying library or country, which should be as simple and clear as possible, must in all cases be observed.

Different practices may be applied to loans and to photocopies or other reproductions sent in place of loans: for example, two countries, or a group of countries, may agree to waive charges for loans but not for photocopies.

11. Statistics

Libraries participating in international lending shall keep statistics of requests received from and sent to other countries, and those satisfied in each case. These statistics shall be sent each year to the national centre or national association for forwarding to the IFLA Office for International Lending.

Commentary

The statistics to be collected should include:

1. The total number of requests sent abroad and the total satisfied a) by loan, b) by photocopy.

2. The total number of requests received from abroad and the total satisfied a) by loan, b) by photocopy.

The above statistics should preferably be kept in rank order by country.

Where it is not possible to collect figures for satisfaction rates over all requests, they may be estimated from sample surveys.

A fuller statement of recommended statistics is given in *IFLA Journal*, volume 3 number 2 1977, page 117–126: International lending statistics.

I.F.L.A. INTERNATIONAL LOAN/PHOTOCOPY REQUEST FORM
FORMULAIRE DE DEMANDE DE PRET/PHOTOCOPIE INTERNATIONAL

Request ref. no/Patron identifier
No. de Commande/identite de lecteur

Borrowing library's address
Adresse de la bibliotheque emprunteuse

Call number
Cot de placement

Needed by
Demande avant

Request for:
Commande de:

☐ Loan
Pret

☐ Photocopy
Photocopie

☐ Microfilm

Report/Reponse

Books: Author, title - **Livres:** Auteur, titre / **Serials:** Title, article title, author - **Periodiques:** Titre, titre de l' article, auteur

☐ Part not held/Volume/fasciscule non detenu

☐ Title not held/nous n'avons pas ce titre

☐ Not traced/Ne figure pas dans cette bibl.

☐ Not for loan/Exclu de pret

☐ Copyright restrictions

☐ Not immediatly available. Reapply in .... weeks
Non disponible actuellement. Renouvelez la
demande dans .... semaines

Place of Publication
Lieu de publication

Publisher
Editeur

Year-Annee	Volume-Tome	Part No.	Pages	ISBN/ISSN

Source of verification/reference
Reference bibliographique/Verification

Lending library's address/adresse de la bibliotheque preteuse

☐ Lent until/Prete jusqu'au ....

☐ Use in library only/A consulter sur placeuniquement

I declare that this publication is required only for the
purpose of research or private study.
Je declare que cette publication n'est demande qu'a des
fins de recherche ou d'etude prive

Signature ....

Date ....

LIST OF COUNTRIES

†   Political changes occurred too recently for entries to be combined.

LISTE DES PAYS

† Les changes politiques se sont passées trop récemment pour réunir les inscriptions.

xvi

LÄNDERVERZEICHNIS

†   Politische Veränderungen sind zu neulich passiert für Eintragungen kombiniert zu werden.

Указатель стран

LISTA DE PAISES

† No podíamos incluir recientes cambios políticos.

ALBANIA

1. Albanian libraries will lend and supply photocopies of items published in Albania. The system is based on the **Bibliografia kombëtare e RPS të Shqipërisë—Libri Shqip dhe Artikujt e periodikut Shqip** (National Bibliography of the People's Republic of Albania—Albanian books and articles in Albanian periodicals) and the catalogues and holdings of the National Library of the People's Republic of Albania.

2. a) Requests for loans should be sent to:

    Bibliothèque Nationale
    Service de Prêt Int
    Tirana   Telephone: 58–87

    Academie des Sciences de la RPS d'Albania
    Bibliothèque
    Tirana   Telephone: 79–61

    Bibliothèque de l'université de Tirana
    Service de Prêt Int
    Tirana   Telephone: 64–87

    Bibliothèque de l'Institut Supériure Agricole
    Kamëz
    Tirana

    b) *Despatch of loans:* Air mail.

    c) *Return of loans:* Air mail.

3. a) Requests for photoduplicated material should be sent to:

    Addresses as in 2a above.

    b) *Despatch of photoduplicated material:* Air mail.

4. *Restrictions:* None.

5. *Request forms accepted:* Only IFLA forms accepted at Bibliothèque de l'Institut Supériure Agricole. IFLA forms preferred at the other libraries.

6. Charges

    a) *Loans:* Free from the Bibliothèque Nationale. The other libraries charge.

    b) *Photoduplicated material:* Free except Academie des Sciences which charges 1 coupon or 10 DM.

    c) *35mm microfilm negative:* ⎤

    d) *35mm positive:* ⎟

    e) Paper copy from microfilm: ⎬ Not applicable.

    f) *Duplicate microfiche:* ⎟

    g) *Paper copy from microfiche:* ⎦

7. Method of payment

    a) *Loans:* Coupons and bills (except the National Library which provides a free service).

    b) *Photoduplicated material:* Coupons and bills (Academie des Sciences only).

8. *Loan period:* One month.

9. *Renewal:* On special occasions and by written request.

1

ALGERIA*

1. The Bibliothèque Nationale and the Bibliothèque Universitaire d'Alger form the 2 centres for international lending in Algeria. There are no union catalogues or printed listings of Algerian publications.

2. a) Requests for loans should be sent to:

    Bibliothèque Nationale d'Algérie
    Service du Prêt Interbibliothèques
    1 Avenue Frantz Fanon
    Alger   **Telephone: 63–06–32, 63–10–49**

    b) *Despatch of loans:* Air mail.

    c) *Return of loans:* Air mail not required.

3. a) Requests for photocopies should be sent to:

    Address as in 2a above.

    b) *Despatch of photocopies:* Air mail

4. *Restrictions:* None.

5. *Request forms accepted:* IFLA forms.

6. Charges

    a) *Loans:* Postage costs not charged. For bibliographic search: 5 International Reply coupons.

    b) *Photoduplicated material:* 1 DA per page.

    c) *35mm microfilm negative:* 0.75 DA per page.

    d) *35mm positive:* 0.75 DA per page.

    e) *Paper copy from microfilm:* 0.75 DA per page.

    f) *Duplicate microfiche:* 30 DA.

    g) *Paper copy from microfiche:* 1 DA per page, 30 DA per fiche.

7. Method of payment

    a) *Loans:* Not applicable.

    b) *Photoduplicated material:* International Reply coupons or Unesco coupons.

8. *Loan period:* 1–3 months.

9. *Renewal:* No restrictions.

ANGOLA

1. The National Library of Angola provides interlending facilities to local and foreign libraries. No union catalogue has been published.

2. a) Requests for loans should be sent to:

    **Biblioteca Nacional
    PO Box 2915
    Luanda**   **Telex: 4129 Secult, AN**

    b) *Despatch of loans:* Air mail and registered.

    c) *Return of loans:* Air mail preferred.

3. a) Requests for photoduplicated material should be sent to:

    Address as in 2a above.

    b) *Despatch of photocopies:* No information given.

4. *Restrictions:* None.

5. *Request forms accepted:* IFLA forms or official letters on headed paper.

6. Charges

    a) *Loans:* Free.

    b) *Photoduplicated material:* Free.

    c) *35mm microfilm negative:*

    d) *35mm positive:*

    e) *Paper copy from microfilm:*   } Not applicable.

    f) *Duplicate microfiche:*

    g) *Paper copy from microfiche:*

7. Method of payment

    a) *Loans:*   } Not applicable.

    b) *Photoduplicated material:*

8. *Loan period:* 4 weeks.

9. *Renewal:* For up to 2 weeks by request.

ANTIGUA

1. There is no national system.

2. There is no loan service.

3. a) Requests for photoduplicated material should be sent to:

OE CS Economic Affairs Secretariat
Documentation Centre
PO Box 822
St Johns
Antigua
West Indies   **Telephone: 462–3500**
                                                  Telex: 2157 Econ Sec AK
                                                  Fax: 462–1537

   b) *Despatch of photoduplicated material:* Air mail.

4. *Restrictions:* Economic affairs relating to member states and the wider Caribbean only.

5. *Request forms accepted:* No information given.

6. Charges

   a) *Loans:* Not applicable.

   b) *Photoduplicated material:* EC$ 0.75 per page.

   c) *35mm microfilm negative:*

   d) *35mm positive:*

   e) *Paper copy from microfilm:* } Not applicable.

   f) *Duplicate microfiche:*

   g) *Paper copy from microfiche:*

7. Method of payment

   a) *Loans:* Not applicable.

   b) *Photoduplicated material:* US$ cheques.

8. *Loan period:* Not applicable.

9. *Renewal:* Not applicable.

ARGENTINA*

1. Loans and photocopies may be requested from the Universidad de Buenos Aires and photocopies only from the Biblioteca Nacional and the Centro Argentina de Información Científica y Tecnólogica (CAICYT). CAICYT specialises in periodical articles. The Biblioteca Nacional is a legal depository library for the country and its stock cannot therefore be lent. The Universidad de Buenos Aires maintains a union catalogue of the holdings of its libraries (1 million cards); a union catalogue of the holdings, 1970 onwards, of the libraries of the other national universities (300,000 cards); and the Argentine Bibliography, a printed union catalogue in 7 volumes of Argentine holdings in the libraries of the Universidad de Buenos Aires, published in 1980. The Centro Argentina de Información Científica y Technólogica (CAICYT) has published a union list of the periodical holdings of scientific and technical libraries.

A. Universidad de Buenos Aires

2. a) Requests for loans should be sent to:

    Universidad de Buenos Aires
    Instituto Bibliotecológico
    Casilla de Correo 901
    1000–Buenos Aires   **Telex: 18694 IBUBA AR**

    b) *Despatch of loans:* Air mail.

    c) *Return of loans:* Air mail.

3. a) Requests for photocopies should be sent to:

    Address as in 2a above.

    b) *Despatch of photocopies:* Air mail.

4. *Restrictions:* Some on manuscripts and theses.

5. Request forms accepted: IFLA forms preferred.

6. Charges

    a) *Loans:*

    b) *Photoduplicated material:*

    c) *35mm microfilm negative:*   Usually no charge but some
                                            libraries may charge in
    d) *35mm positive:*   certain circumstances.

    e) *Paper copy from microfilm:*

    f) *Duplicate microfiche:*

    g) *Paper copy from microfiche:*

7. Method of payment:

    a) *Loans:*   Usually no charge. No
                                            additional information given.
    b) *Photoduplicated material:*

8. *Loan period:* One month.

9. *Renewal:* No significant restrictions.

10. *Additional information:* Loans should be sent and returned direct to the supplying library—the Instituto Bibliotecológico acts as a coordinating centre for all the libraries of the Universidad de Buenos Aires.

B. Biblioteca Nacional

2. There is no loan service.

3. a) Requests for photocopies should be sent to:

    Biblioteca Nacional
    México 564
    1097 Buenos Aires

    b) *Despatch of photocopies:* Air mail not used.

4. *Restrictions:* No items are lent.

5. *Request forms accepted:* No information given.

6. Charges

    a) *Loans:* Not applicable.

    b) *Photoduplicated material:* $US 0.25 per page.

    c) *35mm microfilm negative:* $US 1.00.

    d) *35mm positive:* $US 1.00.

    e) *Paper copy from microfilm:*

    f) *Duplicate microfiche:*   No information given.

    g) *Paper copy from microfiche:*

7. Method of payment

    a) *Loans:* Not applicable.

    b) *Photoduplicated material:* Bank draft/cheque to:

      'Amigos Biblioteca Nacional'
      México 564
      1097 Buenos Aires

8. *Loan period:*

             Not applicable.

9. *Renewal:*

C.   Centro Argentino de Información Científica y Tecnólogica (CCAICYT)

2. There is no loan service.

3.   a) Requests for photocopies should be sent to:

    Centro Argentino de Información Científica y Tecnólogica (CAICYT)
    Moreno 431
    1091 Buenos Aires

3–9. No further information given.

AUSTRALIA

1. The interlibrary loan system in Australia is based on voluntary cooperation by libraries working according to the principles set out in the *Australian Interlending Code of the Australian Council of Libraries and Information Services (ACLIS)*. Copies of the code are available on request from the Document Supply Service, National Library of Australia, Canberra ACT 2600 Australia.

Libraries should make requests to a library known to hold the item required. Where locations are not known, an overseas library is invited to approach the Document Supply Service of the National Library of Australia. Where the National Library is unable to supply a loan or copy of an Australian item, it will search appropriate union catalogues and forward the overseas request to another Australian library that holds the item and will notify the requesting library. This service is not offered to libraries in New Zealand or New Guinea which are situated close to Australia and use the Document Supply Service on a regular basis. Leaflets on the Document Supply Service are available from the National Library.

The main part of the Australian National Union Catalogue is based on the National Bibliographic Database, accessible through the Australian Bibliographic Network (ABN) and its products.

The major serial union list, **NUCOS**, is a product of ABN, and is currently available in COM-fiche. The major monograph union list, **NUCOM**, is partly available in microfilm, and partly available in COM-fiche.

Information on NUCOS, NUCOM, and other parts of the National Union Catalogue are available from the National Library.

2. a) Requests for loans should be sent to:

> **Document Supply Service**
> **National Library of Australia**
> **Canberra ACT 2600**
> **Australia**
>
> Telephone: 61–62–621438
> Telex: AA62100 LIBAUST
> Fax: 61–62–732719

  b) *Despatch of loans:* Air mail.

  c) *Return of loans:* Air mail.

3. a) Requests for photoduplicated materials should be sent to:

  Address as in 2a above.

  b) *Despatch of photoduplicated material:* Air mail.

4. *Restrictions:* Periodicals, Australian deposit items and printed issues of newspapers are not for loan. Other items may not be available for loan due to rarity, value, poor condition or some other consideration.

5. *Request forms accepted:* Australian Standard ACLIS—approved request forms, IFLA request forms or American Library Association request forms.

6. Charges

  a) *Loans:* $A 6.00 per item.

  b) *Photoduplicated material:* ($A 6.00 per item (by post))
  ($A 6.00 per page (by fax))

  c) *35mm microfilm negative:*

  d) *35mm positive:*

  e) *Paper copy from microfilm:*   No information given.)

  f) *Duplicate microfiche:*

  g) *Paper copy from microfiche:*

7. Method of payment

  a) *Loans:*   Payment in advance is preferred. Regular users may purchase prepayment vouchers from the Document Supply Service.

  b) *Photoduplicated material:*

8. *Loan period:* 5 weeks.

9. *Renewal:* Automatically granted unless the item is required by another user.

AUSTRIA

1. For each county ('Bundesland') there exists at least one leading library ('Leitbibliothek') that is responsible for bibliographical verification of the requests it receives from the libraries of its region. They should be fulfilled by the holdings of the Leitbibliothek or other libraries of this county. Otherwise they can be passed on to other Austrian libraries according to guidelines written down in the *'Österreichische Fernleiheordnung' (ÖFLO)*. Copies of the ÖFLO can be obtained from the Österreichische Nationalbibliothek.

   Passing on of requests and purposeful ordering is also made possible according to locations found in the 2 union-catalogues, one for periodicals and one for monographs:

   ## ÖSTERREICHISCHE ZEITSCHRIFTENDATENBANK (ÖZDB).
   A database of periodicals (foreign and Austrian) in Austrian libraries. Also available on microfiche and CD-ROM.

   ## Katalog der BÜCHERNACHWEISSTELLE.
   Union catalogue of monographs published 1930–1980 in foreign countries. The holdings of all important Austrian research-libraries with the exception of the Österreichische National-bibliothek. Available as microfiche-edition. The publications 1981 onwards exist as a card-catalogue held at the Österreichische Nationalbibliothek solely.

   The Österreichische Nationalbibliothek acts as a centre for international lending as far as Austrian documents are concerned.

2. a) Requests for loans should be sent to:

   Österreichische Nationalbibliothek
   Fernleihe
   Josefsplatz 1
   A-1015 Wien   **Telephone: 53410/275**
                           Telex: 112624 (oenb a)
                           Fax: 533 70 49

   b) *Despatch of loans:* Registered printed paper.

   c) *Return of loans:* Air mail not required.

3. a) Requests for photoduplicated material should be sent to:

   Address as in 2a above.

   b) *Despatch of photoduplicated material:* Air mail not used to European countries.

4. *Restrictions:* No loans outside Europe. Newspaper, journals, pre-1850 material and special collections not lent. Photoduplication restrictions are possible for conservation reasons.

5. *Request forms accepted:* IFLA forms only.

6. Charges

   a) *Loans: Postal costs.*

   b) *Photoduplicated material:* No charge made for up to 10 items. More than 10 items: invoice for all copies plus postal and packaging costs.

   c) *35mm microfilm negative:* ⎫
   d) *35mm positive:*   ⎬ Price list available.
   e) *Paper copy from microfilm:* ⎪
   f) *Duplicate microfiche:*   ⎭

   g) *Paper copy from microfiche:* 4. Schillings per copy.

7. Method of payment

    a) *Loans:* International reply coupons

    b) *Photoduplicated material:* Invoice

8. *Loan period:* 4 weeks.

9. *Renewal:* One renewal for 4 weeks.

BAHAMAS

1. There is no national system

2.   a) Requests for loans should be sent to:

      Nassau Public Library
      PO Box N-3210, 809
      322–4907
      Nassau   **Telephone: 809 322–4907**

      The College of the Bahamas
      PO Box N-4912
      Nassau   **Telephone: 809 323–7930–2**
                                809 323–8550–2
                         Fax: 809 326–7834

    b) *Despatch of loans:* Air mail.

    c) *Return of loans:* Air mail.

3.   a) Requests for photoduplicated material should be sent to:

      Addresses as in 2a above.

    b) *Despatch of photoduplicated material:* Air mail.

4. *Restrictions:* Bahamian material is not loaned. However, specific details may be duplicated.

5. *Request forms accepted:* ALA interlibrary request forms.

6. Charges

    a) *Loans:* Postal costs.

    b) *Photoduplicated material:* B.25 cents (Letter size)
                                    B.30 cents (A3 size)

    c) *35mm microfilm negative:* ⎫
                                      ⎬ Not applicable.
    d) *35mm positive:* ⎭

    e) *Paper copy from microfilm:* B.15 cents.

    f) *Duplicate microfiche:* ⎫
                                    ⎬ Not applicable.
    g) *Paper copy from microfiche:* ⎭

7. Method of payment

    a) *Loans:* Postal slips.

    b) *Photoduplicated material:* Money order.

8.   *Loan period:* 2 weeks.

9.   *Renewal:* Granted on request.

BAHRAIN

1.   There is no interlending system and no national library.

BANGLADESH

1.   There is no formal national system and no union catalogue has been produced yet.

      The newly established National Library of Bangladesh provides interlending facilities to local libraries for all materials in its stock.

2.   a)   Requests for loans should be sent to:

            Assistant Director
            National Library of Bangladesh
            She-e-Bangla Nagar, (Agargaon)
            Dhaka-1207

      b)   *Despatch of loans:* Air mail unless otherwise requested.

      c)   *Return of loans:* Air mail.

3.   a)   Requests for photoduplicated material should be sent to:

            Address as in 2a above.

      b)   *Despatch of photoduplicated material:* Air mail.

4.   *Restrictions:* Single copy items and rare books are not lent.

5.   *Request forms accepted:* IFLA forms.

6.   Charges

      a)   *Loans:* Free.

      b)   *Photoduplicated material:* One taka.

      c)   *35mm microfilm negative:*

      d)   *35mm positive:*

      e)   *Paper copy from microfilm:*   Not applicable

      f)   *Duplicate microfiche:*

      g)   *Paper copy from microfiche:*

7.   Method of payment

      a)   *Loans:* Not applicable.

      b)   *Photoduplicated material:* Cheque.

8. *Loan period:* Flexible.

9. *Renewal:* On request.

BARBADOS*

1. The system is based on the recently established Barbados Library Archive and Information Centre Network (BLAIN).

2. The Network's address is:

    Barbados Library Archive and Information Centre Network (BLAIN)
    Bay Street
    St Michael

3–9 No further information given.

BELGIUM

1. No formal national or international lending system exists in Belgium. Requests from abroad may be sent to whichever library is preferred by the borrowing library.

    There exists a transportation system elaborated by the main university libraries and some research libraries, which communicates the books between these libraries.

    The Vrije Universiteit Brussel is the focus of the system. The members of the system adhere to a number of regulations.

    The Royal Library is mainly a reference library but it accepts to lend to research and special libraries. Several libraries come to the Royal Library to collect the books they have requested. Because of the small size of Belgium and the central geographic situation of the Royal Library this practice is efficient.

    The Royal Library lends to important public libraries geographically spread all over Belgium.

    In the Flemish part of Belgium a regulation exists concerning loan traffic between public libraries.

    There are 2 main union catalogues for periodicals:

    —Antilope: lopende periodieken aanwezig in Belgische universitaire, wetenschappelijke en speciale bibliotheken. 5th edition. Antwerpen, 1987, 1110 p. (32,861 titles, 73,237 holdings).

    This is an inventory of current periodicals in Belgian special and scientific libraries.

    —Catalogue collectif belge et luxembourgeois des périodiques étrangers en cours de publication. Belgische en Luxemburgse centrale catalogus van lopende buitenlandse tijdschriften. Cockx, A. (ed), Brussel, 1965, 2 vols:

    Suppl 1: 1975: 9 microfiches

    Suppl 2: 1979: 13 microfiches

    This catalogue is outdated but still useful.

    The Université catholique de Louvain (UCL) edited a Union catalogue of biomedical periodicals in Belgian Universities:

    Inventaire permanent des périodiques biomédicaux en cours en Belgique. 5e ed. Louvain, 1989.

In 1989 ORDA-B, under the direction of the Universities of Gent and Leuven, produced a union catalogue of monographs on CD-ROM. This catalogue gives access to 2,700,000 publications. A second and enlarged edition is planned for 1992.

Several University libraries and scientific libraries connected by LIBIS network have access to a union catalogue.

Antwerp universities have access to their own catalogue, as they are linked by VUBIS network.

Flemish public libraries make use of an online union catalogue (VLACC). This catalogue is also available on CD-ROM.

2. a) Requests for loans should be sent to:

Universitaire Instelling Antwerpen
Universiteitsplein 1
Postbus 13
B—2610 Wilrijk   **Telephone: 03 820–21–41**
                                                Telefax: 03 827–08–74

Université libre de Bruxelles
Avenue F D Roosevelt 50
B—1050 Bruxelles   **Telephone: 02 642–39–60**
                                                Telefax: 02 642–35–95

Vrije Universiteit Brussel
Pleinlaan 2
B—1050 Brussel   **Telephone: 02 641–25–03**
                                                Telefax: 02 641–22–82

Rijksuniversiteit Gent
Rozier 9
B—9000 Gent   **Telephone: 091 25–75–71**
                                                Telefax: 091 25–80–92

Katholieke Universiteit Leuven
Centrale Bibliotheek
Mgr Ladeuzeplein 21
B—3000 Leuven   **Telephone: 016 28–46–06**
                                                Telefax: 016 28–46–16

Université catholique de Louvain
Centre général de documentation
Place Cardinal Mercier 31
B—1348 Louvain-la-Neuve   **Telephone: 010 47–48–48**
                                                Telefax: 010 47–28–91

b) *Despatch of loans:* Surface mail in Europe; usually air mail elsewhere.

c) *Return of loans:* Items sent by air mail must be returned by air mail.

3. a) Requests for photoduplicated material should be sent to:

Addresses as in 2a above.

b) *Despatch of photoduplicated material:* Surface mail in Europe; usually air mail elsewhere.

4. *Restrictions:* As a general rule there are no significant restrictions on certain categories of material for loan except for books considered to be reference works and for periodicals published within the last 10 years. These periodicals will be supplied only in the form of photocopies.

5. *Request forms accepted:* IFLA forms preferred.

6. Charges

a) *Loans:* No uniform price. The Royal Library charges postage costs only.

12

b) *Photoduplicated material:* No uniform price. Most university and scientific libraries charge 175 BF per article (up to 30 pages) and 5 or 6 BF per additional page. For telefax most university and scientific libraries charge 500 BF per article (up to 10 pages) and 50 BF per additional page.

c) *35mm microfilm negative:*

d) *35mm positive:*

e) *Paper copy from microfilm:* } No uniform price.

f) *Duplicate microfiche:*

g) *Paper copy from microfiche:*

7. Method of payment

a) *Loans:*

b) *Photoduplicated material:* } Invoice or international coupons. Some libraries ask for pre-payment (depending on the amount).

8. *Loan period:* Usually one month but this may be restricted in the case of frequently used material.

9. *Renewal:* Renewals are accepted if no local reader has reserved the book and provided the renewal request arrives before the expiration of the first loan period.

10. *Additional information:* As there is no national centre all material should be sent/returned directly to the library concerned.

BELIZE

1. There is no national system.

2. There is no loan service.

3 a) Requests for photoduplicated material should be sent to:

National Library Service
PO Box 287
Belize City

b) *Despatch of photoduplicated material:* No information given.

4. *Restrictions:* No information given.

5. *Request forms accepted:* No information given.

6. Charges

a) *Loans:* Not applicable.

b) *Photoduplicated material:* Free

c) *35mm microfilm negative:*

d) *35mm positive:*

e) *Paper copy from microfilm:* } Not applicable.

f) *Duplicate microfiche:*

g) *Paper copy from microfiche:*

7. Method of payment

   a) *Loans:*

   b) *Photoduplicated material:* } Not applicable.

8. *Loan period:* Not applicable.

9. *Renewal:* Not applicable.

BERMUDA

1. Bermuda Library and Bermuda College lend materials nationally and internationally.

2. a) Requests for loans should be sent to:

   Interlibrary Loan
   Bermuda Library
   13 Queen Street
   Hamilton
   HM11   **Telephone: 809–295–3104**

   Bermuda College
   POB DV 356
   Devonshire
   DV BX   **Telephone: 809–292–5205**

   b) *Despatch of loans:* Air and surface mail.

   c) *Return of loans:* Air mail if despatched by air mail.

3. a) Requests for photoduplicated material should be sent to:

   Addresses as in 2a above.

   b) *Despatch of photoduplicated material:* Air mail.

4. *Restrictions:* Reference and rare book material are not lent (Bermuda Library). Reference material is not lent (Bermuda College).

5. *Request forms accepted:* IFLA forms.

6. Charges

   a) *Loans:* Charges.

   b) *Photoduplicated material:* 25 cents per copy.

   c) *35mm microfilm negative:* 50 cents per copy.

   d) *35mm positive:* 50 cents per copy.

   e) *Paper copy from microfiche:* 25 cents per copy.

   f) *Duplicate microfiche:*

   g) *Paper copy from microfiche:* } Not applicable.

7. Method of payment

   a) *Loans:*

   b) *Photoduplicated material:* } Cheques payable to 'Accountant General—Bermuda'

14

8. *Loan period:* 28 days.

9. *Renewal:* Allowable.

BOTSWANA

1. Botswana does not have a formal interlending system within the country and has no union catalogue. Both the Botswana National Library Services and the University Library are members of the Southern African Libraries interlending system. Thus the Interlibrary Loans Manual for Southern African Libraries published by the State Library, PO Box 397, Pretoria is used as a guideline. The University of Botswana Library is the national centre for processing loans outside the Southern African Libraries system and deals mainly with the British Library Document Supply Centre.

2. a) Requests for loans should be sent to:

   University of Botswana Library
   Private Bag 0022
   Gaborone   **Telephone: Gaborone 351151**

   b) *Despatch of loans:* Air mail.

   c) *Return of loans:* Air mail.

3. a) Requests for photoduplicated material should be sent to:

   Address as in 2a above.

   b) *Despatch of photoduplicated material:* No information given.

4. *Restrictions:* No information given.

5. *Request forms accepted:* IFLA forms.

6. Charges

   a) *Loans:* Charges

   b) *Photoduplicated material:*

   c) *35mm microfilm negative:*   No information given.

   d) *35mm positive:*

   e) *Paper copy:*

   f) *Duplicate microfiche:* R 12.00

   g) *Paper copy from microfiche:* No information given.

7. Method of payment

   a) *Loans:* Cash.

   b) *Photoduplicated material:* Coupons.

8. *Loan period:* No information given.

9. *Renewal:* Allowable.

10. Additional information: To date, Botswana uses the international lending system sparingly, probably due to the well established regional schemes, which satisfy most of their requests.

BRAZIL

1. There is no national system. The National Library does not provide national or international interlending facilities but it provides copying facilities. Two union catalogues are available. The **Catálogo Coletivo Nacional de Periódicos Brasileiros** (National Union Catalogue of Brazilian Serials) is published by the Instituto Brasileiro de Informação em Ciência and Technología. **Periódicos Brasileiros em Microformas** (Brazilian Serials in Microforms) is published by the National Library.

2. No loan service.

3. a) Requests for photoduplicated material should be sent to:

   Biblioteca Nacional
   Av Rio Branco 219/239
   20042–Rio de Janeiro, RJ   **Telephone: 021 2409229**
                                                Telex: 212294/BNRJ-BR

   Instituto Brasileiro de Informaçâo em Ciência and Tecnologia
   SCN Quadra 2 Bloco K
   70710 Brasilia-DF   **Telephone: 061 2255192**
                                                Telex: 612481

   b) *Despatch of photoduplicated material:* Air mail.

4. *Restrictions:* Material is photoduplicated or microfilmed according to its state of conservation. Pre-1900 material can only be microfilmed.

5. *Request forms accepted:* Official letters on headed paper or standard international request forms such as IFLA forms.

6. Charges

   a) *Loans:* Not applicable.

   b) *Photoduplicated material:* US$0.12 per page.

   c) *35mm negative microfilm:* US$0.12 per page for general collection and US$0.24 per page for rare books collection.

   d) *35mm positive microfilm:* US$0.24 per page for general collection and US$0.47 per page for rare books collection.

   e) *Paper copy from microfilm:* Size A2—US$2.32, Size 3 US$1.16, Size A4—US$0.58.

   f) *Duplicate microfiche:*   ⎫
                                          ⎬ Not applicable.
   g) *Paper copy from microfiche:*   ⎭

7. Method of payment

   a) *Loans:* Not applicable.

   b) *Photoduplicated material:* Cheques payable to Fundaçâo Nacional Pro-Leitura/Biblioteca Nacional.

8. *Loan period:* Not applicable.

9. *Renewal:* Not applicable.

10. *Additional information:* Although the National Library policy does not allow an international loan service, the Library will provide some material on special occasions through national and international agreements.

BULGARIA

1. The Cyril and Methodius National Library is the national centre for national and international lending. The system is governed by Guidelines for National Interlending in Bulgaria as approved by the Committee of Culture in Sofia 1987 and by IFLA regulations of 1974. In addition other libraries function as centres for international lending and also provide on request certain types of reprographic copies eg xerox copies, microfilms etc. Loan requests may be sent to all of them either by letter or by telex. There is no special procedure for telex requests. There are two major union catalogues in Bulgaria: one for foreign books published after 1944 and held by major and research libraries and one for foreign periodicals currently received by the same libraries.

2. a) Requests for loans should be sent to:

    Cyril and Methodius National Library
    Boul. Tolbuhin 11
    1504 Sofia   Telephone: 88–28–11, extensions 252 & 293
                                           Dept of International Lending
                                           Telex: 22432 NATLIB

    Central Library of the Bulgarian Academy of Sciences
    7 Noemvri 1
    1000 Sofia   Telephone: 8–4141, ext 257
                                           Telex: 22424

    University Library
    Boul. Ruski 15
    1504 Sofia   Telephone: 85–81, ext 554

    Central Library for Science and Technology
    Boul. Nasser 50
    1040 Sofia   Telephone: 70–29–78
                                           Telex: 22404

    Central Library of Agriculture
    Boul. Lenin 125 bl. 1
    1113 Sofia   Telephone: 7–43–71, ext 541

    Central Library of Medicine
    Georgi Sofijski 1
    1431 Sofia   Telephone: 53–21

    Ivan Vasov Library
    NJ Vapcarov 17
    4000 Plovdiv   Telephone: 2–29–15, ext 19

    b) *Despatch of loans:* Air mail; usually registered.

    c) *Return of loans:* Air mail.

3. a) Requests for photoduplicated material should be sent to:

    Addresses as in 2a above.

    b) *Despatch of photoduplicated material:* Registered surface mail.

4. *Restrictions:* Excluded from international lending are old and rare books, (but reprographic copies are possible) materials of a size inconvenient for despatch, and expensive books containing plates and illustrations.

5. *Request forms accepted:* The latest IFLA form is preferred.

6. Charges

    a) *Loans:* Postage only.

b) *Photoduplicated material:* Postage plus Leva 0.10 per page.

c) *35mm microfilm negative:* Leva 0.14 per page for 1 to 3 pages. Leva 0.07 per page for each additional page.

d) *35mm positive:* Leva 0.28 per page for 1 to 3 pages. Leva 0.14 per page for each additional page.

e) *Paper copy from microfilm:* Size 9/14: Leva 0.30.
    Size 13/18: Leva 0.50.
    Size 18/24: Leva 0.70.

f) *Duplicate microfiche:* Leva 1.80.

g) *Paper copy from microfiche:* Leva 0.40 per page.

7. Method of payment

    a) *Loans:*

    b) *Photoduplicated material:* } International reply coupons, cheque or bank remittance.

8. *Loan period:* One month.

9. *Renewal:* On request.

BURUNDI*

2. There is no loan service.

3. a) Requests for photoduplicated material should be sent to:

    Université Officielle de Bujumbura
    Bibliothèque Centrale
    B.P. 1320
    Bujumbura

    b) *Despatch of photoduplicated material:* Air mail.

4. *Restrictions:* No significant restrictions.

5. *Request forms accepted:* Any.

6. Charges

    a) *Loans:* Not applicable.

    b) *Photoduplicated material:* FBU 20 per page.

    c) *35mm microfilm negative:*

    d) *35mm positive:*

    e) *Paper copy from microfilm:* } No information given.

    f) *Duplicate microfiche:*

    g) *Paper copy from microfiche*

7. Method of payment

   a) *Loans:* Not applicable.

   b) *Photoduplicated material:* Payment should be made to the account of the University of Burundi No: 1101/27/Université du Burundi at the Banque de la République du Burundi.

8. *Loan period:* ⎫
              ⎬ Not applicable
9. *Renewal:* ⎭

CAMEROON

1. There is no organized system for interlending in the country, but the University Library fulfils this function when requested to do so.

2. a) Requests for loans should be sent to:

   University Library
   P.O. Box 1312
   Yaoundé   **Telex: 8384 KN**

   b) *Despatch of loans:* Air mail

   c) *Return of loans:* Air mail

3. a) Requests for photoduplicated material should be sent to:

   Address as in 2a above.

   b) *Despatch of photoduplicated material:* Air mail

4. *Restrictions:* None

5. *Request forms accepted:* IFLA forms or letters

6. Charges

   a) *Loans:* Postage costs.

   b) *Photoduplicated material:* 50 Frs per page

   c) *35mm microfilm negative:* ⎫

   d) *35mm positive:* ⎪

   e) *Paper copy from microfilm:* ⎬ Not applicable

   f) *Duplicate microfiche:* ⎪

   g) *Paper copy from microfiche:* ⎭

7. Method of payment

   a) *Loans:* ⎫
                               ⎬ International Reply Coupons
   b) *Photoduplicated material:* ⎭

8. *Loan period:* One month

9. *Renewal:* Loans may be automatically extended by two weeks, if late in arriving.

CANADA

1. The interlending system in Canada is decentralised. Libraries outside Canada wishing to borrow books from Canadian libraries may address the library known to hold the item directly. When locations are not known, the National Library of Canada will act as a clearinghouse for interlibrary loan requests in the humanities and social sciences from other countries, referring such requests to appropriate Canadian sources when material cannot be supplied from the library's collection. Scientific requests should be sent directly to the Canada Institute for Scientific and Technical Information (CISTI).

    Interlending in Canada is supported by a variety of on-line and published union catalogues. Union catalogues published on microfiche include: **Union List of Serials in the Social Sciences and Humanities in Canadian Libraries, Union List of Canadian Newspapers**, and the **Canadian Union Catalogue of Library Materials for the Handicapped** (CANUC:H) which are available from the Government Publishing Centre, Ottawa, Canada K1A OS9; and the **Union List of Scientific Serials in Canadian Libraries** which is available from CISTI.

    The CLA/ASTED Interlibrary Loan Code which sets out the principles for interlibrary loan in Canada, and the CLA/ASTED Interlibrary Loan Procedures Manual can be obtained from the Canadian Library Association, 200 Elgin Street, Ottawa, Ontario K2P 1L5. The French versions can be obtained from Secretariat de l'ASTED, 1030 rue Cherrier, Bureau 505, Montreal, Quebec H2L 1H9.

    More detailed information on the services of the National Library of Canada and CISTI's services is available upon request (see address below).

A. National Library of Canada

2. a) Requests for loans should be sent to:

    Interlibrary Loan Division
    National Library of Canada
    395 Wellington Street
    Ottawa
    Ontario
    K1A ON4

    Telephone: (613)-996–3566
    Telex: 053–4311 NATLIB OTT
    Envoy 100: Compose ILL (Script)

    b) *Despatch of loans:* Air mail.

    c) *Return of loans:* Air mail preferred.

3. a) Requests for photoduplicated material should be sent to:

    Address as in 2a above.

    b) *Despatch of photoduplicated material:* Air mail. If requested, copies can be sent by telefacsimile.

4. *Restrictions:* Tapes, records and originals of newspapers are not lent.

5. *Request forms accepted:* IFLA forms preferred.

6. Charges

    a) *Loans:* Free.

    b) *Photoduplicated material:*

    c) *35mm microfilm negative:*

    d) *35mm positive:*

    e) *Paper copy from microfilm:* } Estimates available on request.

    f) *Duplicate microfiche:*

    g) *Paper copy from microfiche:*

7. Method of payment

    a) *Loans:* Not applicable.

    b) *Photoduplicated material:* Monthly invoices are despatched.

8. *Loan period:* 4 weeks.

9. *Renewal:* Not available on newspaper microfilms.

B. Canada Institute for Scientific and Technical Information (CISTI)

2. There is no loan service outside Canada.

3.   a) Requests for photoduplicated material should be sent to:

    Canada Institute for Scientific and Technical Information
    Document Delivery
    Ottawa
    Canada
    K1A OS2   **Telephone: (613) 993–1585**
                                  Telex: 053–3115 NRC CISTI OTT

    b) *Despatch of photoduplicated material:* Air mail.

4. *Restrictions:* None.

5. *Request forms accepted:* Standard 3 part ILL forms (one part of the form is required for invoicing).

6. Charges

    a) *Loans:* Not applicable.

    b) *Photoduplicated material:* $10 Cdn for every 10 pages.

    c) *35mm microfilm negative:*

    d) *35mm positive:* } Not applicable.

    e) *Paper copy from microfilm:* $10 Cdn for every 10 pages.

    f) *Duplicate microfiche:* $10 Cdn per document.

    g) *Paper copy from microfiche:* $10 Cdn for every 10 pages.

7. Method of payment

    a) *Loans:* Not applicable.

    b) *Photoduplicated material:* Deposit accounts or monthly invoice.

8. *Loan period:*

           } Not applicable.

9. *Renewal:*

CHAD

1.	There is no national interlibrary lending system. At the level of N'Djaména, by an agreement between libraries, services are made available to readers coming from one or other of the following three libraries—the University, ENS and ENAM.

CHILE

1.	There is no official procedure for international interlibrary loan fundamentally because of the lack of sufficient copies and because of the unreliability of means of communication added to a certain percentage of non-cooperation amongst the participants. At a national level it functions particularly between academic libraries.

2.	There is no loan service.

3.	a)	Requests for photoduplicated material should be sent to:

	Biblioteca Nacional, Coordinación General
	Canada 308
	Casilla 297–V
	Santiago

	b)	*Despatch of photoduplicated material:* Air mail.

4.	*Restrictions:* Date of printing and physical state.

5.	*Request forms accepted:* IFLA forms.

6.	Charges

	a)	*Loans:* Not applicable.

	b)	*Photoduplicated material:* US$ 3.00 for 1–10 photocopies. US$ 0.30 for each additional photocopy.

	c)	*35mm microfilm negative:*

	d)	*35mm positive:* ⎫ No information given.

	e)	*Paper copy from microfilm:*

	f)	*Duplicate microfiche:* $35 (letter size).

	g)	*Paper copy from microfiche:* $40 (double letter size).

7.	Method of payment

	a)	*Loans:* Not applicable.

	b)	*Photoduplicated material:* US dollar cheque made out to the Biblioteca Nacional.

8.	*Loan period:* ⎫
	                  ⎬ Not applicable.
9.	*Renewal:* ⎭

PEOPLE'S REPUBLIC OF CHINA

1. The system is based on the union catalogues supported by the collections of the National Library of China and a few large libraries in China.

A. National Library of China

2. a) Requests for loans should be sent to:

   Interlibrary Loans
   National Library of China
   39 Baishiqiao Road
   Beijing 100081   **Telephone: 831–6355**

   b) *Despatch of loans:* Air mail.

   c) *Return of loans:* Air mail.

3. a) Requests for photoduplicated material should be sent to:

   Address as in 2a above.

   b) *Despatch of photoduplicated material:* Air mail.

4. *Restrictions:* Newspapers, reference books, maps, rare books, thread-bound Chinese books and others not suitable for postal handling are not lent.

5. *Request forms accepted:* IFLA forms preferred.

6. Charges

   a) *Loans:* Charges are waived by mutual agreement.

   b) *Photoduplicated material:*
   c) *35mm microfilm negative:*
   d) *35mm positive:* } 1–10 pages: $7.50.
   e) *Paper copy from microfilm:*

   f) *Duplicate microfiche:*
   g) *Paper copy from microfiche:* } No information given.

7. Method of payment

   a) *Loans:* See 6a.

   b) *Photoduplicated material:* Cheque sent by registered mail or bank draft.

8. *Loan period:* One month from date of receipt.

9. *Renewal:* Renewals of 2 weeks will be granted unless the item is required by another user.

10. *Additional information:* Each item or part-item must be requested on a separate request form.

B.   Resource Information Centre for Chinese Studies*

2.   No information regarding a loan service was received.

3.   a)   Requests for photoduplicated material should be sent to:

**Liaison Division
Resource and Information Centre for Chinese Studies
43 Nan-hai Road
Taipei**

b)   *Despatch of photoduplicated material:* Air mail.

4.   *Restrictions:*

5.   *Request forms accepted:*   No information given.

6.   Charges

a)   *Loans:* No information given.

b)   *Photoduplicated material:* Up to 10 pages: US$3.00 } Including
                                  Up to 20 pages: US$5.00 } postage.
                                  Over 20 pages: US$5.00, plus $0.10 per page, plus postage.

c)   *35mm microfilm negative:*

d)   *35mm positive:*

e)   *Paper copy from microfilm:*   No information given.

f)   *Duplicate microfiche:*

g)   *Paper copy from microfiche:*

7.   Method of payment

a)   *Loans:*

b)   *Photoduplicated material:*

8.   *Loan period:*   No information given.

9.   *Renewal:*

COLOMBIA

1.   There is no national system. The address of the National Library is:

**Biblioteca Nacional de Colombia
Calle 24 No. 5–60
Bogota**

CONGO*

1.   The system is based on union catalogues.

2.   There is no loan service.

3.   a)   Requests for photoduplicated material should be sent to:

   Bibliothèque Universitaire
   B.P. 20.25
   Brazzaville

   b)   *Despatch of photoduplicated material:* Air mail.

4.   *Restrictions:* None.

5.   *Request forms accepted:* Any.

6.   Charges

   a)   *Loans:*

   b)   *Photoduplicated material:*

   c)   *35mm microfilm negative:*

   d)   *35mm positive:*

   e)   *Paper copy from microfilm:*

   f)   *Duplicate microfiche:*   } No information given.

   g)   *Paper copy from microfiche:*

7.   Method of payment

   a)   *Loans:*

   b)   *Photoduplicated material:*

8.   *Loan period:*
                   } Not applicable.
9.   *Renewal:*

COOK ISLANDS

1.   There is no national system.

2.   a)   Requests for loans should be sent to:

   Cook Islands Library
   P.O. Box 71
   Rarotonga   **Telephone 26–468**

   b)   *Despatch of loans:* Air mail and registered.

   c)   *Return of loans:* Air mail and registered.

3. a) Requests for photoduplicated material should be sent to:

   Address as in 2a) above.

   b) *Despatch of photoduplicated material:* Air mail if required urgently.

4. *Restrictions:* Books from the Rare Book Pacific Collection are not loaned. Old books are not photocopied.

5. *Request forms accepted:* No information given.

6. Charges

   a) *Loans:* Postage costs.

   b) *Photoduplicated material:* 15 cents (New Zealand currency) per page (A4 and foolscap).

   c) *35mm microfilm negative:*
   d) *35mm positive:* } Not applicable.

   e) *Paper copy from microfilm:* 15 cents per page.

   f) *Duplicate microfiche:*
   g) *Paper copy from microfiche:* } Not applicable.

7. Method of payment

   a) *Loans:*
   b) *Photoduplicated material:* } Bank draft in New Zealand currency.

8. *Loan period:* 1 month.

9. *Renewal:* No information given.

10. *Additional information:*

   The library is prepared to assist any requests for materials in their Pacific Reference Collection that can be copied. It will also act as a contact for those libraries wishing to acquire materials from the Cook Islands especially government publications.

COSTA RICA

1. There is no national system. The address of the national library is:

   Biblioteca Nacional
   Apdo. 100008
   Calle 5
   Avdas 1/3
   San José

CÔTE D'IVOIRE

1. There is no national system. The address of the national library is:

   Bibliothèque Nationale
   BPV 180
   Abidjan   **Telephone: 32–38–72**

CUBA

1. There is no national system but the Biblioteca Nacional José Martí acts as a centre for interlending activity.

2. a) Requests for loans should be sent to:

   Biblioteca Nacional José Martí
   Grupo Catálogo Colectivo y Préstamo Interbibliotecario
   Ciudad Habana   **Telephone: 70–8157**
   79–6091–98 Ext 17
   Telex: 0511963

   b) *Despatch of loans:* Air mail.

   c) *Return of loans:* Air mail preferred.

3. a) Requests for photoduplicated material should be sent to:

   Address as in 2a above.

   b) *Despatch of photoduplicated material:* Air mail.

4. *Restrictions:* Rare and valuable documents; audiovisual material.

5. *Request forms accepted:* Any.

6. Charges

   a) *Loans:* Free.

   b) *Photoduplicated material:* ⎤
   c) *35mm microfilm negative:* ⎟
   d) *35mm positive:* ⎟ Documents are requested in
   e) *Paper copy from microfilm:* ⎬ exchange, according to the
   f) *Duplicate microfiche:* ⎟ value of the item sent.
   g) *Paper copy from microfiche:* ⎦

7. Method of payment

   a) *Loans:* ⎤
   b) *Photoduplicated material:* ⎦ Not applicable

8. *Loan period:* 3 months.

9. *Renewal:* No restrictions.

CZECHOSLOVAKIA

1. There is a decentralised system in Czechoslovakia (ČSSR) based on several libraries in the Czech Socialist Republic (ČSR) and the Slovak Socialist Republic (SSR). The State Library of the ČSR, Praha, is the national centre for Czech and Czechoslovak Literature, based on a legal deposit collection of material published in Bohemia and Czechoslovakia and on union catalogues of foreign literature held in Czechoslovakia (monographs after 1950; periodicals up to 1964). The State Library, Praha, acts also on behalf of the following libraries, which participate in international lending in the Czech Socialist Republic: ÚVTEI-Státní technická knihovna, Praha; ÚVI-Základni knihovna ČSAV, Praha; Státní vědecká knihovna, Brno; Státní vědecká knihovna, Olomouc.

    The University Library, Bratislava, is the national centre for Slovak and Czechoslovak literature, based on a legal deposit collection of material published in Slovakia and Czechoslovakia and on the union catalogues of foreign literature held in Czechoslovakia (monographs after 1950, periodicals after 1965). As well as the University Library Bratislava, the Central Library of the Slovak Academy of Sciences, Bratislava, and the Slovak Technical Library, Bratislava, participate in international lending in the Slovak Socialist Republic.

2. a) Requests for loans should be sent to:

    Státní knihovna ČSR
    Klementinum 190
    CS 110 01 Praha 1   **Telephone: 23 58 727, 26 65 41**
                                                Telex: 12 12 07 STKN C

    Univerzitná knižnica
    Michalská 1
    CS 814 17
    Bratislava   **Telephone: 33 32 47, 33 11 51**
                                                Telex: 93 255 UNKZ C

    Slovenská technická knižnica
    Gottwaldovo nám. 19
    CS 812 23
    Bratislava   **Telephone: 513 84**
                                                Telex: 93 230 SLTKC

    Slovenská akadémia vied
    ústr knižnica
    Klemensova 19
    CS 814 67   **Telephone: 563 21**
                                                Telex: 92764 UKSAV C

    Requests may be sent with the agreement of the library concerned direct to a holding library:

    ÚVTEI-Státní technická knihovna
    nam. dr. Vacka 2
    CS 113 07 Praha 1   **Telephone: 26 53 73**

    ÚVI-Zakladní knihovna ČSAV
    Národní 3
    CS 115 22 Praha 1   **Telephone: 25 65 65**

    Státní vědecká knihovna
    Leninova 5–7
    CS 601 87 Brno   **Telephone: 72 75 00**
                                                Telex: 62 299 SVKBR C

    Státní vědecká knihovna
    Bezručova 2
    CS 771 77 Olomouc   **Telephone: 23 441**

b) *Despatch of loans:* Registered surface mail within Europe unless air mail is specified. Generally air mail outside Europe.

c) *Return of loans:* Air mail not required.

3. a) Requests for photoduplicated material should be sent to:

Addresses as in 2a above.

b) *Despatch of photoduplicated material:* Registered surface mail.

4. *Restrictions:*

The following categories of material are not lent: manuscripts; printed matter of historical, bibliographical or artistic value; legal deposit copies printed in Czechoslovakia and abroad; rare and precious books; dissertations; newspapers and maps.

The following items are not photocopied (xerox): manuscripts, rare and precious books, legal deposit copies of artistic value, newspapers, maps, some dissertations.

Manuscripts will not be microfilmed unless approved by the relevant authority.

5. *Request forms accepted:* IFLA forms preferred

6. Charges

a) *Loans:* No charge. Postage costs are, in most cases, recovered on a reciprocal basis.

b) *Photoduplicated material:* Up to 10 pages free, thereafter 1,50 Kčs per A4 page.

c) *35mm microfilm negative:* 1,40 Kčs per frame.

d) *35mm positive:* 0.70 Kčs per frame.

e) *Paper copy from microfiche:* Per A5 page 2,00 Kčs
Per A4 page 3,20 Kčs
Per A3 page 5,20 Kčs

f) *Duplicate microfiche:* 4,00 Kčs ⎫
⎬ State Library of ČSR only.
g) *Paper copy from microfiche:* 3,00 Kčs) ⎭

7. Method of payment

a) *Loans:* International Reply Coupons.

b) *Photoduplicated material:* International Reply Coupons.

8. *Loan period:* One month from date of receipt (2 weeks for periodicals).

9. *Renewal:* Allowable unless required by another reader.

10. Additional information

It is particularly emphasised that requests for Czech and Slovak items should give a precise transcription complete with diacritic signs of the original bibliographic details, and the source of reference should be quoted wherever possible. Diacritic signs are crucial for Czech and Slovak titles, since their presence or absence considerably alters the place of the title in the alphabetical sequence. Similarly, titles should not be abbreviated by the requesting library.

Matica slovenská, Martin (National Library of Slovak Socialist Republic) does not directly participate in the international cooperation of interlending and document delivery. Its library holdings serve as a deposit collection of Slovak and Czechoslovak literary production and the documents on Slovakia published in foreign countries. Matica slovenská builds up also the literary archive. Services of Matica slovenská can be used through the National center of interlending and document delivery in the Slovak Socialist Republic.

DENMARK

1. The system is generally decentralised, based on a network of public libraries and research libraries. All Danish publications are collected according to the Legal Deposit Act by Det kongelige Bibliotek (the Royal Library), Statsbiblioteket (the State and University Library) in Århus and the Universitetsbibliotekets 1 afdeling (University Library, Humanities Section), in Copenhagen.

   The Danish Loan Centre (DABL) is placed at the State and University Library in Århus. The Loan Centre receives requests for Danish material from abroad, but it is also possible to send requests for non-Danish material to the Centre where they will be checked in the catalogues at DABL and then forwarded to location traced.

   There is one union catalogue for non-Danish material in the research libraries, started 1901, online from 1981, in the base called ALBA, and one union catalogue for non-Danish material in public libraries from 1972, online in the base called BASIS. These two online systems also give locations for a great part of Danish material published as from 1980.

2. a) Requests for loans should be sent to:

   Statsbiblioteket
   (State and University Library)
   Danish Loan Centre
   Universitetsparken
   DK-8000 Århus C   Telephone: + 45 86 12 20 22
                                           Telex: 64515 (stabib dk)
                                           Fax: + 45 86 13 72 07

   b) *Despatch of loans:* Air mail.

   c) *Return of loans:* Air mail not required.

3. a) Requests for photoduplicated material should be sent to:

   Address as in 2a above.

   b) *Despatch of photoduplicated material:* Air mail.

4. *Restrictions:* No special restrictions on photoduplication. Certain categories of material are retained for use in the library.

5. *Request forms accepted:* IFLA forms required.

6. Charges

   a) *Loans:* Free.

   b) *Photoduplicated material:* 1,00 DKr per copy.

   c) *35mm microfilm negative:* 2,00 DKr per exposure.

   d) *35mm positive:* 25,00 DKr per meter.

   e) *Paper copy from microfilm:* 1,50 DKr per copy.

   f) *Duplicate microfiche:* Not applicable.

   g) *Paper copy from microfiche:* 1,50 DKr per copy.

7. Method of payment

   a) *Loans:* Not applicable.

   b) *Photoduplicated material:* Cheque, postal cheque service or bank transfer.

8. *Loan period:* One month.

9. *Renewal:* Granted unless the item is required by another reader.

10. *Additional information:* Statsbiblioteket, Danish Loan Centre, is the Danish national loan centre.

FAROE ISLANDS

1. There is no national system. Loan requests should be sent to the National Library.

2. a) Requests for loans should be sent to:

   Føroya Landsbokasavn
   J C Svabosgøta 16
   FR-110 Torshavn   **Telefax; tel: 1 1626 (domestic)**

   b) *Despatch of loans:* Air mail.

   c) *Return of loans:* No particular requirements.

3. a) Requests for photoduplicated material should be sent to:

   Address as in 2a above.

   b) *Despatch of photoduplicated material:* Air mail.

4. *Restrictions:* None.

5. *Request forms accepted:* Any.

6. Charges

   a) *Loans:*

   b) *Photoduplicated material:*   } Free

   c) *35mm microfilm negative:*

   d) *35mm positive:*

   e) *Paper copy from microfilm:*

   f) *Duplicate microfiche:*   } No charges yet.

   g) *Paper copy from microfiche:*

7. Method of payment

   a) *Loans:*   } Not applicable.

   b) *Photoduplicated material:*

8. *Loan period:* 1 month.

9. *Renewal:* Allowed.

10. *Additional information:* All requests for material should be sent to the National Library and all items returned to it.

DOMINICA

1. The National Library Service provides a lending service to all its branch libraries and other libraries operating in the country. It also participates in interlending schemes with other regional information services eg Infonet CARISPLAN—ECLAC, U.W.I., CAGRIS and on an informal basis with other national libraries in the Eastern Caribbean sub region.

2. a) Requests for loans should be sent to:

    The Documentation Centre
    Roseau   **Telephone: 82401**

    b) *Despatch of loans:* Air mail.

    c) *Return of loans:* Air mail.

3. a) Requests for photoduplicated material should be sent to:

    Address as in 2a above.

    b) *Despatch of photoduplicated material:* Air mail.

4. *Restrictions:* Government restricted documents.

5. *Request forms accepted:* IFLA forms.

6. Charges

    a) *Loans:* Postal costs for material outside OECS.

    b) *Photoduplicated material:* 35cEC per page.

    c) *35mm microfilm negative:* ⎫
    d) *35mm positive:* ⎭ Not applicable.

    e) *Paper copy from microfilm:* 15 USc per page.

    f) *Duplicate microfiche:* ⎫
    g) *Paper copy from microfiche:* ⎭ Not applicable.

7. Method of payment

    a) *Loans:* ⎫
    b) *Photoduplicated material:* ⎭ Postal money orders or cheques in US dollars

8. *Loan period:* 2 months.

9. *Renewal:* Allowed if the publication is not requested by another user.

EGYPT*

1. There is no international loan service. Photoduplicated material may be obtained from the National Library.

2. There is no loan service.

3. a) Requests for loans should be sent to:

   Egyptian National Library
   GEBO Corniche El Nil-Boulac
   Cairo

   b) *Despatch of photoduplicated material:* Air mail.

4. *Restrictions:*

5. *Request forms accepted:*
   } No information given.

6. Charges

   a) *Loans:* Not applicable.

   b) *Photoduplicated material:* 20 Egyptian piasters per page.

   c) *35mm microfilm negative:* Not applicable.

   d) *35mm positive:* $0.50.

   e) *Paper copy from microfilm:*

   f) *Duplicate microfiche:*
   } Not applicable.

   g) *Paper copy from microfiche:*

7. Method of payment

   a) *Loans:* Not applicable.

   b) *Photoduplicated material:* No information given.

8. *Loan period:*

9. *Renewal:*
   } Not applicable.

ETHIOPIA*

1. The system is based on Addis Ababa University Libraries from which details of services may be obtained.

2. a) Requests for loans should be sent to:

    Kennedy Library
    Gifts and Exchange Section
    Addis Ababa University Libraries
    PO Box 1176
    Addis Ababa   **Telephone: 11–56–73**
                                                       Telex: 21205

    b) *Despatch of loans:* Air mail.

    c) *Return of loans:* Air mail.

3. a) Requests for photoduplicated material should be sent to:

    Address as in 2a above.

    b) *Despatch of photoduplicated material:* Air mail.

4–9. No further information was supplied for the 3rd edition. However, the second edition gave the following information:

4. *Restrictions:* Rare national material is not lent but photocopies can be supplied at cost.

5. *Request forms accepted:* Any.

6. Charges

    a) *Loans:* Refund of postage required.

    b) *Photoduplicated material:* Charged by invoice.

    c) *35mm microfilm negative:*

    d) *35mm positive:*

    e) *Paper copy from microfilm:*

    f) *Duplicate microfiche:*   No information given.

    g) *Paper copy from microfiche:*

7. Method of payment

    a) *Loans:*

    b) *Photoduplicated material:*

8. *Loan period:* One month from date of receipt.

9. *Renewal:* Not allowed.

FIJI

1. The system is based on the main Library and the agriculture library of the University of the South Pacific. International lending arrangements exist with New Zealand, Australia, UK and South Pacific Island libraries. The main union catalogue is the **South Pacific Union List of Periodicals**.

2. a) Requests for loans should be sent to:

    Interlibrary Loan (Library)
    University of the South Pacific Library
    PO Box 1168
    Suva
    Fiji Islands   **Telephone: 313900 extension 284 or 27225**
                                             Telex: 2276 USP FJ
                                             Cables: University Suva
                                             Fax: (679) 300830

    The Librarian
    School of Agriculture
    University of the South Pacific
    PO Box 890
    Apia
    Western Samoa   **Telephone: 21671**
                                             Telex: 251 USP SX
                                             Cables: University Apia
                                             Fax: (683) 22933

    b) *Despatch of loans:* Second class air mail.

    c) *Return of loans:* Air mail.

3. a) Requests for photoduplicated material should be sent to:

        Addresses as in 2a above.

    b) *Despatch of photoduplicated material:* Second class air mail.

4. *Restrictions:* Materials from the Pacific Collection, reference collection, periodicals and theses are not loaned.

5. *Request forms accepted:* Most types are acceptable.

6. Charges

    a) *Loans:* Free.

    b) *Photoduplicated material:* 6 cents per page.

    c) *35mm microfilm negative:* ⎫
                                   ⎬ Not applicable.
    d) *35mm positive:*   ⎭

    e) *Paper copy from microfilm:* 40 cents per page.

    f) *Duplicate microfiche:* Not applicable.

    g) *Paper copy from microfiche:* 40 cents per page.

7. Method of payment

    a) *Loans:* Not applicable.

    b) *Photoduplicated material:* Cheque, purchase order, or postal order.

8. *Loan period:* 30 days from the date of postage.

9. *Renewal:* Allowed unless materials are required by USP or regional patrons.

FINLAND

1. The system is based on a network of central research libraries, other research libraries and public libraries. There is no central interlending library; every library has to be approached separately.

Addresses of research libraries, industrial libraries and more important public libraries are to be found in **Suomen tieteellisten kirjastojen opas** (Guide to Research Libraries and Information Services in Finland), ed Matti Liinamaa and Annikki Hokynar, Helsinki, 7th edition (New edition under preparation).

The main union catalogue for monographs is **Suomen tieteellisten kirjastojen ulkomaisen kirjallisuuden yhteisluettelo** (Union Catalogue of Foreign Literature in Research Libraries in Finland). After 1975 there are three parallel versions on microfiche;

i) an annual version of the union catalogue... A. Books;

ii) Finuc—ISBN catalogue, 1975 cumulation;

iii) The union catalogue/D80, 1980 cumulation.

Used parallel with written catalogues and microfiches there are databases for locating information:

KATI for articles and special bibliographies (since 1982);

KOTI for the national bibliography (since 1977);

KAUKO for foreign literature in research libraries acquired after 1980 (since 1982); and

KAUSI for Finnish and foreign periodicals in Finnish and other Nordic research libraries (since 1985);

MUSA for music recordings (since 1985).

National interlending guidelines are available in Finnish and are also translated into Swedish.

2. a) Requests for loans should be sent to:

(i) For Finnish material:

Turku University Library
Interlending
Yliopistonmäki
20500 Turku   Telephone: + 358 21 645 179
                                      Telex: 62123 tyk sf

This library supplies loans in the Finnish language.

Library of Åbo Academy
Interlending
Tuomiokirkkokatu 2–4
20500 Turku   Telephone: + 358 21 654 311
                                      Telex: 62301 aabib sf

This library supplies loans of publications in the Swedish language, published in Finland.

(ii) Non-Finnish material:

Requests for non-Finnish material should be sent to the central research libraries. (See 1 above for the publication which lists the addresses).

b) *Despatch of loans:* Air mail.

c) *Return of loans:* Air mail may be required (depends on the requirements of the supplying library).

3. a) Requests for photoduplicated material should be sent to:

(i) For Finnish material:

Addresses as in 2ai above.

Turku University library supplies photoduplicated material in the Finnish language. The Library of the Åbo Academy supplies photoduplicated material of publications, translations etc in the Swedish language, published in Finland.

(ii) Non-Finnish material:

Central research libraries as in 2aii above.

b) *Despatch of photoduplicated material:* Air mail.

4. *Restrictions:* The following categories of material are not available for loan but may be supplied as photocopies: newspapers, unbound periodicals, periodicals published within the last ten years, bibliographies, reference works, university course literature, valuable or worn books.

5. *Request forms accepted:* IFLA forms preferred.

6. Charges

a) *Loans:* Free.

b) *Photoduplicated material:* A small charge.

c) *35mm microfilm negative:* ⎫
d) *35mm positive:* ⎭ Not applicable.

e) *Paper copy from microfilm:* ⎫
f) *Duplicate microfiche:* ⎬ A small charge.
g) *Paper copy from microfiche:)* ⎭

7. Method of payment

a) *Loans:* Not applicable.

b) *Photoduplicated material:* Invoice or deposit account.

8. *Loan period:* 1 month. In special cases a shorter loan period may be stipulated.

9. *Renewal:* Where possible renewals are made.

10. *Additional information:* Helsinki University Library acts as the National Library of Finland but does not lend Finnish material.

FRANCE

1. The system is based on the Centre de Prêt de la Bibliothèque Nationale, the Institut National de l'Information Scientifique et Technique (INIST) of the Centre National de la Recherche Scientifique (CNRS) and the Centres d'Acquisition et de Diffusion de l'Information Scientifique of Technique (CADIST). The Centre de Prêt de la Bibliothèque Nationale acts as the international interlending centre and will forward requests it cannot satisfy to other libraries in France. The CNRS does not lend but supplies photocopies from its stock of periodicals, conference proceedings, research reports and scientific theses. The CADIST form an organisation set up by the Sous-Direction des Bibliothèques, in which certain university libraries act as a centre of last resort in a specific subject field. There is a national union list of serials **Catalogue Collectif National (CCN)**, an on-line catalogue of 460,000 titles; and a union catalogue of foreign books, **Catalogue Collectif des ouvrages étrangers (CCOE)**. The CNRS publishes a catalogue of periodicals received annually.

National guidelines for interlending were published in 1981 for university libraries; new guidelines for all libraries should be available from early 1984.

A. Centre de Prêt de la Bibliothèque Nationale.

2. a) Requests for loans should be sent to:

        Centre de Prêt de la Bibliothèque Nationale
        Réf. post 1101
        78011 Versailles Cedex   **Telephone: (1) 39–51–67–98**
                                            Telex: 696492 BNPRET

    b) *Despatch of loans:* Air mail to most overseas countries and on request.

    c) *Return of loans:* Loans supplied by air mail must be returned by air mail.

3. a) Requests for photoduplicated material should be sent to:

    Address as in 2a above.

    b) *Despatch of photoduplicated material:* Air mail to most overseas countries and on request.

4. *Restrictions:* Newspapers and rare books are not photocopied. In such cases a microfiche may be lent if such already exists or a reproduction made on request and with prepayment.

5. *Request forms accepted:* IFLA forms.

6. Charges

    a) *Loans:* Surface mail: 33,30 FF or 1 vignette BN or 10 International reply coupons. Air mail: 66,60 FF or 2 vignettes BN or 20 International reply coupons.

    b) *Photoduplicated material:* 1–10 pages: 33,30 FF or 1 vignette BN or 10 International reply coupons. 11–20 pages: 66,60 FF or 2 vignettes BN or 20 International reply coupons. 21–50 pages: 99,90 FF or 3 vignettes BN or 30 International reply coupons.

    c) *35mm microfilm negative:*

    d) *35mm positive:*   Not applicable.

    e) *Paper copy from microfilm:*   Microfiche are sent on loan only.

    f) *Duplicate microfiche:*

    g) *Paper copy from microfiche:*

7. Method of payment

    a) *Loans:*   Prepayment is required by means of BN vignette. A set of 20 vignettes costs 666 FF. Without vignette, payment can be effected by international reply coupons, by a cheque payable in a French bank, or by bank transfer to the: Recette Générale des Finances de Paris, 19, rue Scribe, 75009 Paris. Order to 'Bibliothèque Nationale':

    b) *Photoduplicated material:*   Account 30081 75000 00004400 911 31

8. *Loan period:* One month.

9. *Renewal:* May be made but application should be made before the end of the existing loan period.

10. *Additional information:* All international requests should be sent to the Centre de Prêt (but see B below).

B. Institut National de l'Information Scientifique et Technique du Centre National de la Recherche Scientifique (INIST/CNRS).

2. There is no loan service.

3. a) Requests for photoduplicated material should be sent to:

    INIST/CNRS
    Service fournitures de documents
    2, allée du Parc de Brabois
    F 54514 Vandoeuvre les Nancy Cedex　　　　**Telephone: (16) 83–50–46–00 poste 7320**
    　　　　　　　　　　　　　　　　　　　　　　　　Telex: 850225F
    　　　　　　　　　　　　　　　　　　　　　　　　Fax: (16) 83–50–46–46

    Requests should be sent by post or on-line, following interrogation of the databases, including PASCAL.

    b) *Despatch of photoduplicated material:* Air mail.

4. *Restrictions:* None.

5. *Request forms accepted:* INIST/CNRS request forms. IFLA forms are not accepted.

6. Charges

    a) *Loans:* Not applicable.

    b) *Photoduplicated material:*

    c) *35mm microfilm negative:*

    d) *35mm positive:*　　　　　　　　　　　Charges are by article and units of 10 pages

    e) *Paper copy from microfilm:*　　　　　 for photocopy, microfilm or microfiche

    f) *Duplicate microfiche:*

    g) *Paper copy from microfiche:*

7. Method of payment

    a) *Loans:* Not applicable.

    b) *Photoduplicated material:* Prepayment is required by means of INIST/CNRS coupons. (Details available on request).

8. *Loan period:*
    　　　　　　　　　Not applicable.
9. *Renewal:*

39

FRENCH GUIANA

1. Please see the entry under FRANCE. There is no local union catalogue.

2. a) Requests for loans should be sent to:

    Bibliothèque Universitaire Antilles-Guyane-Section Guyane
    B.P 718
    97300 Cayenne   **Telephone: 594 31.94.60**

    b) *Despatch of loans:* Air mail.

    c) *Return of loans:* Air mail.

3. a) Requests for photoduplicated material should be sent to:

    Address as in 2a above.

    b) *Despatch of photoduplicated material:* Air mail.

4. *Restrictions:* Cetain exceptions (unspecified).

5. *Request forms accepted:* IFLA forms.

6. Charges

    a) *Loans:* Postal costs.

    b) *Photoduplicated material:* 1–10 pages: 40,70F. Additional 1–10 pages: 20,40F.

    c) *35mm microfilm negative:*

    d) *35mm positive:*

    e) *Paper copy from microfilm:* } Not applicable.

    f) *Duplicate microfiche:*

    g) *Paper copy from microfiche:*

7. Method of payment

    a) *Loans:*   } International money order or coupons of
    b) *Photoduplicated material:*   } the Universal Posal Union.

8. *Loan period:* One month.

9. *Renewal:* Allowed on request if the book is not needed by anybody else.

MARTINIQUE

1. National and international interlending is performed by the Bibliothèque Universitaire Antilles-Guyane.

2. a) Requests for loans should be sent to:

    **Bibliothèque Universitaire Antilles-Guyane/Service de
    Prêt entre Bibliothèques
    B.P. 7210
    97275 Schoelcher Cedex**

    b) *Despatch of loans:* Air mail.

    c) *Return of loans:* Air mail.

3. a) Requests for photoduplicated material should be sent to:

    Address as in 2a above.

    b) *Despatch of photoduplicated material:* Air mail.

4. *Restrictions:* None of significance.

5. *Request forms accepted:* Any.

6. Charges

    a) *Loans:* Postal costs.

    b) *Photoduplicated material:* 1 Franc per page.

    c) *35mm microfilm negative:*

    d) *35mm positive:*

    e) *Paper copy from microfilm:* } No information given.

    f) *Duplicate microfiche:*

    g) *Paper copy from microfiche:)*

7. Method of payment

    a) *Loans:*
    } Unesco coupons.
    b) *Photoduplicated material:*

8. *Loan period:* About three weeks from date of receipt.

9. *Renewal:* Allowed on request.

RÉUNION

1. The University Library provides interlending facilities to local libraries.

2. a) Requests for loans should be sent to:

    Université de La Réunion
    Service Commun de la Documentation
    Prêt Inter
    97489—Saint Denis Cedex
    France

    Telephone: 19 (262) 28–1873
    20.20.07
    Fax: 29–17–00
    Telex: 916 6H5 RE

    b) *Despatch of loans:* Air mail or Chronopost (Express service).

    c) *Return of loans:* Air mail.

3. a) Requests for photoduplicated material should be sent to:

    Address as in 2a above.

    b) *Despatch of photoduplicated material:* Air mail.

4. *Restrictions:* Books from the Reserve will only be lent if a duplicate copy exists. Photocopies or microfilms may be supplied at cost.

5. *Request forms accepted:* IFLA forms.

6. Charges

    a) *Loans:* Postage costs.

    b) *Photoduplicated material:* No information given.

    c) *35mm microfilm negative:* Price available on request.

    d) *35mm positive:* No information given.

    e) *Paper copy from microfilm:* ⎫
    f) *Duplicate microfiche:* ⎬ French rate.

    g) *Paper copy from microfiche:* F.F 2,50.

7. Method of payment

    a) *Loans:* ⎫
    b) *Photoduplicated material:* ⎬ Cheques or stamps.

8. *Loan period:* One month.

9. *Renewal:* Not allowed.

THE GAMBIA

1.   There is no national system. The National Library is for reference only. Its address is:

National Library
Independence Drive
P.O.Box 552
Banjul

GERMAN DEMOCRACTIC REPUBLIC

1.   The system is based on five interlending regions of the German Democratic Repulic, supported by union catalogues (national and regional). Requests which cannot be satisfied by one region will be passed on to another.

   The Deutsche Staatsbibliothek acts as a centre for international loans only for requests sent from libraries of the GDR to foreign libraries.

   Copies of the national guidelines may be obtained from the Deutsche Staatsbibliothek.

   The unification of Germany will affect its interlending systems but political events have been too recent for any changes to be included in this Guide.

2.   a)   Requests for loans should be sent to:

Deutsche Staatsbibliothek
Institut für Leihverkehr und Zentralkataloge
DDR 1086 Berlin
Unter den Linden 8
Postfach-Nr. 1312   **Telex: 112 023 STABI DD**
                                         112 757 STABI DD

   The above library acts as a national co-ordinating centre for international loans.

Sächsische Landesbibliothek
DDR 8060 Dresden
Marienallee 12, PSF 467   **Telex: 2368 LABI DD**

Universitäts- und Landesbibliothek
Sachsen-Anhalt
DDR 4010 Halle
August-Bebel-Str. 13 und 50   **Telex: 4252 ULB HAL DD**

Universitätsbibliothek
DDR 6900 Jena
Goetheallee 6   **Telex: 5886134 UNI DD**

Universitätsbibliothek
DDR 7010 Leipzig
Beethovenstrasse 6   **Telex: 51345 UNIBIB DD**

Universitätsbibliothek
DDR 2500 Rostock
Universitätsplatz 5   **Telex: 31140 UNIR DD**

   b)   *Despatch of loans:* Air mail to countries outside Europe.

   c)   *Return of loans:* Air mail preferred from countries outside Europe.

3. a) Requests for photoduplicated material should be sent to:

    Addresses as in 2a above.

   b) *Despatch of photoduplicated material:* Surface mail to Europe, air mail outside Europe.

4. *Restrictions:* Newspapers, journals, large format or heavy, old and or valuable books, reading room works and reference works for official use are not lent. Photocopies or microfilms of single articles can be supplied (articles from newspapers only exceptionally).

5. *Request forms accepted:* IFLA forms preferred.

6. Charges

   a) *Loans:* Postage charges can be waived by mutual agreement.

   b) *Photoduplicated material:*

    Xerox copy:

Basic fee	M 4,00
From originals up to A3, per A4 copy	M 0,60
Per copy larger than A3	M 0,90
From originals larger than A3, per copy	M 3,50

   and c) d) *Microfilm:*

    Silver-halide unperforated roll from originals up to A3:

Basic fee	M 2,00
32 x 22,5mm per frame	M 0,90
32 x 45,0mm per frame	M 1,10
From originals larger than A3, per frame	M 3,50

    Copying on 35mm silver film:

Basic fee	M 2,00
32 x 22,5mm per frame	M 0,30
32 x 45,0mm per frame	M 0,45

   e) *Paper copy from microfilm:* No information given.

   f) *Duplicate microfiche:*

Basic fee per fiche	M 2,00
Original negative A6, 21 × reduction per fiche	M 25,00
Diazo duplicate negative or positive per fiche	M 3,50
Positive copy on silver film per fiche	M 5,00

   g) *Paper copy from microfiche:* No information given.

7. Method of payment

   a) *Loans:* International Reply Coupons are preferred for loan postal costs.

   b) *Photoduplicated material:* Invoices are sent with the goods. Payment may be made by bank draft or crossed cheque.

8. *Loan period:* One month from date of receipt.

9. *Renewal:* Available unless the item is required by another user.

FEDERAL REPUBLIC OF GERMANY

1.   The system is based on seven interlending regions of the German Federal Republic. In each region one central catalogue lists the holdings of libraries within that region. Various subject union catalogues provide further guidance. An online union list of serials is found in the form of the **Zeitschriftendatenbank: ZDB-Gesamtausdruck, Stand 4/89, Berlin, Deutsches Bibliotheksinstitut, 1989. ISBN 3–447–08448–0**, available on microfiche. There also exists **GesamtKatalog (GK)**. Most of the union catalogues and the GK are available on microfiche and some of them have online connections. International lending is co-ordinated by the Clearingstelle für den Internationalen Leihverkehr of the Staatsbibliothek Preussischer Kulturbesitz, but requests may be made direct to a library specialising in the subject concerned, where one is known. A list of these 44 subject specialised libraries and guidelines for international lending may be obtained from the 'Clearingstelle' at the address below. A further guide to interlending in the Federal Republic of Germany is:

Die Ordnung des Leihverkehrs in der Bundesrepublik Deutschland. Text und Kommentar der Leihverkehrsordnung von 1979: Ed. Sinogowitz, Bernhard and Kratsch, Werner. Frankfurt am Main, Klostermann, 1982, ISBN 3–465–0151–0. (Zeitschrift für Bibliotheksewesen und Bibliographie, Sonderheft 35), DM 40.

The Zentralbibliothek der Medizin acts as the National Medical Library of the FRG. As the national document supply centre for biomedical literature it collects and supplies scientific literature in medicine and related fields and delivers it to libraries in the country and abroad as well as to users directly.

The unification of Germany will affect the library systems but events have been too recent for any changes to be included in this Guide.

A.   Staatsbibliothek Preussischer Kulturbesitz.

2.   a)   Requests for loans should be sent to an appropriate centre (see 1 above) or to:

        Staatsbibliothek Preussischer Kulturbesitz
        Clearingstelle für den Internationalen Leihverkehr
        Postfach 1407
        D-1000 Berlin 30   **Telex: 183 160 staab d**
                                    Telefax: 030 266 2814

    b)   *Despatch of loans:* Air mail only if required and paid for by the requesting library.

    c)   *Return of loans:* Items sent by air mail should be returned by air mail.

3.   a)   Requests for photoduplicated material should be sent to:

        Address as in 2a above.

    b)   *Despatch of photoduplicated material:* Only sent overseas by air mail.

4.   *Restrictions:* If for some reason an item is unavailable for loan, photocopies are made available.

5.   *Request forms accepted:* IFLA forms preferred.

6.   Charges

    For requests of literature published in Germany (loan or copy) usually no fees are charged.

    a)   *Loans:* DM 10,00 per unit   } (For literature published
    b)   *Photoduplicated material:* 1–20 pages: DM 10,00   outside Germany)

    c)   *35mm microfilm negative:*   }
                                       Charges vary
    d)   *35mm positive:*   }

    e)   *Paper copy from microfilm:* 1–20 pages: DM 10,00

f) *Duplicate microfiche:* 1–5 fiches: DM 10,00 ⎫ (For literature published
g) *Paper copy from microfiche:*1–20 pages: DM 10,00 ⎭ outside Germany)

7. Method of payment

   a) *Loans:* ⎫ Cumulative invoices are sent.
   b) *Photoduplicated material:* ⎭ Payment may be made by coupons or remittance.

8. *Loan period:* One month.

9. *Renewal:* One month's renewal is available.

10. *Additional information:* The Deutsche Bibliothek in Frankfurt am Main supplies loans and photodupli-cated material as a last resort only.

B. Zentral Bibliothek Der Medizin

2. a) Requests for loans should be sent to:

   Zentralbibliothek der Medizin
   Joseph-Stelzmann-Str 9
   D-500 Koeln 41   **Telephone: 49 221 4785608**
                                   Telefax : 49 221 4785697
                                   Telex : 88 2214 zbme d

   b) *Despatch of loans:* A charge is made for air mail.

   c) *Return of loans:* Air mail not required.

3. a) Requests for photoduplicated material should be sent to:

   Address as in 2a.

   b) *Despatch of photoduplicated material:* A charge is made for air mail.

4. *Restrictions:* Books older than 80 years and periodicals in high demand.

5. *Request forms accepted:* IFLA forms only.

6. *Charges:*

   a) *Loans:* DM 10,00 (if the book is not in German or published in Germany).

   b) *Photoduplicated material:* 1–20 photocopies: DM 10,00.

   c) *35mm microfilm negative:* 1–20 exposures: DM 10,00.

   d) *35mm positive:* Not available.

   e) *Paper copy from microfilm:* 1–20 photocopies: DM 10,00.

   f) *Duplicate microfiche:* DM 10,00 per unit.

   g) *Paper copy from microfiche:* 1–20 photocopies: DM 10,00.

7. Method of payment

   a) *Loans:* ⎫ Semi-annual invoicing when the declaration form issued by
   b) *Photoduplicated material:* ⎬ the Clearingstelle für den Internationalen Leihverkehr/Staatsbib-liothek Preussischer Kulturbesitz is enclosed. Otherwise orders are rejected.

8. *Loan period:* Usually one month but 2 weeks for some material.

9. *Renewal:* Allowable.

10. *Additional information:* Direct orders may be placed by any customer. Special Services eg Urgent Action and Telefax are available; special charges apply then.

GHANA

1. There is no central lending collection, nor are there union catalogues of books. There are, however, two Union Lists of periodicals: (1) **Union List of African and related journals held in the Balme Library, Legon, the Institute of African Studies Library also Legon and the Research Library on African Affairs, Ghana Library Board, Accra 1966**. (2) **Union List of Scientific Serials in Ghanaian Libraries 1976**. Both lists are being revised and updated.

2. a) Requests for loans should be sent to:

   The Balme Library
   University of Ghana
   P.O. Box 24
   Legon, Accra   **Telephone: 775309**

   Council for Scientific and Industrial Research (CSIR)
   P.O. Box M 32
   Accra

   The Library
   University of Science and Technology
   Kumasi

   The Library
   University of Cape Coast
   University Post Office
   Cape Coast

   b) *Despatch of loans:* Air mail.

   c) *Return of loans:* Air mail.

3. a) Requests for photoduplicated material should be sent to:

   Addresses as in 2a above, plus:

   Research Library on African Affairs
   Ghana Library Board
   P.O. Box 663
   Accra

   b) *Despatch of photoduplicated material:* Air mail.

4. *Restrictions:* Serials, theses/dissertations, reference collections are not lent. Photocopies of articles etc can be supplied subject to the usual copyright restrictions.

5. *Request forms accepted:* Any accepted but IFLA or British Library International Loan request forms are preferred.

6. Charges

   a) *Loans:* Free.

   b) *Photoduplicated material:*
      i) Non-library material—C 40.00 per page
      ii) Library material   —C 30.00 per page)
                     [US$1.00 = C270.00 approximately]

   c) *35mm microfilm negative:*

   d) *35mm positive:*

   e) *Paper copy from microfilm:*   } Not applicable.

   f) *Duplicate microfiche:*

   g) *Paper copy from microfiche:*

7. Method of payment:

   a) *Loans:* Not applicable.

   b) *Photoduplicated material:* Invoices are sent with the material and payment should be by crossed cheque. Unesco Book Coupons or British Library Document Supply Centre coupons are also acceptable.

8. *Loan period:* Six weeks.

9. *Renewal:* Allowed unless item is requested by another reader.

GIBRALTAR

1. There is no national system.

2. There is no loan service.

3. a) Requests for photoduplicated material should be sent to:

   Garrison Library
   P.O. Box 374

   b) *Despatch of photoduplicated material:* Air mail.

4. *Restrictions:* None.

5. *Request forms accepted:* Any.

6. Charges

   a) *Loans:* Not applicable.

   b) *Photoduplicated material:* 20p per page.

   c) *35mm microfilm negative:*

   d) *35mm positive:*

   e) *Paper copy from microfilm:* } Not applicable.

   f) *Duplicate microfiche:*

   g) *Paper copy from microfiche:*

7. Method of payment

   a) *Loans:* Not applicable.

   b) *Photoduplicated material:* Invoice

8. *Loan period:*

   } Not applicable.

9. *Renewal:*

GREECE

1. There is no organised interlending in Greece. Requests may be sent direct to individual libraries, although the University of Thessaloniki Library is prepared to act as a centre for international requests. There is no national union catalogue and there are no national guidelines.

2. a) Requests for loans should be sent to:

    University of Thessaloniki Library
    Thessaloniki
    54006 Greece   **Telephone: 031–992860**

    b) *Despatch of loans:* Air mail.

    c) *Return of loans:* Air mail.

3. a) Requests for photoduplicated material should be sent to:

    Address as in 2a above.

    b) *Despatch of photoduplicated material:* Air mail.

4. *Restrictions:* Manuscripts, old material, reference books, and periodicals are not lent.

5. *Request forms accepted:* IFLA forms preferred.

6. Charges

    a) *Loans:* Postage costs are recovered for loans (5 International Reply Coupons for a normal book).

    b) *Photoduplicated material:* 10 drachmas per page or 1 International Reply Coupon per unit of 3 pages.

    c) *35mm microfilm negative:*

    d) *35mm positive:*

    e) *Paper copy from microfilm:*   } No information given.

    f) *Duplicate microfiche:*

    g) *Paper copy from microfiche:*

7. a) *Loans:* International Reply Coupons.

    b) *Photoduplicated material:* International Reply Coupons or cheque.

8. *Loan period:* One month.

9. *Renewal:* One month's renewal granted on request.

GRENADA

1. There is no national system and no national library.

GUINEA

1. There is no interlending system at present but the National Library hopes to establish an international lending system. The address is:

   Bibliothèque Nationale de Guinea
   B.P. 561
   Conakry

GUYANA

1. The system is based on major libraries cooperating informally.

2. a) Requests for loans should be sent to:

   The Librarian
   University of Guyana
   Library
   P.O. Box 101110
   Georgetown   **Telephone: 54841–9 Extension 439**

   The Librarian
   National Library
   P.O. Box 10240
   Georgetown   **Telephone: 62690 or 62699**

   b) *Despatch of loans:* Air mail if requested.

   c) *Return of loans:* Air mail.

3. a) Requests for photoduplicated material should be sent to:

   Addresses as in 2a above.

   b) *Despatch of photoduplicated material:* Air mail if requested.

4. *Restrictions:* Serials are not lent. An explanatory letter is required for photocopying rare and out of print material at both libraries listed.

5. *Request forms accepted:* Any.

6. Charges

   a) *Loans:* Postal charges only.

   b) *Photoduplicated material:* G$ 2.50 per page (University of Guyana).

   G$ 4.00 or US$ 0.15 per page (National Library).

   No concession is made for large quantities of photocopies or for type of paper used whether foolscap size or letter size.

   c) *35mm microfilm negative:*

   d) *35mm positive:*

   e) *Paper copy from microfilm:* } Not applicable.

   f) *Duplicate microfiche:*

   g) *Paper copy from microfiche:*

7. Method of payment

   a) *Loans:* Free except postage refund.

   b) *Photoduplicated material:* Cheque.

8. *Loan period:* By arrangement.

9. *Renewal:* Allowed by special request providing the material is not requested by local users in Guyana.

10. *Additional information:* The University of Guyana also acts as a referral centre. If requests are made for material which is not part of its collection, it will refer the request to the library which holds the requested material.

HAITI

1. There is no national system. The address of the National Library is:

   Bibliothèque Nationale
   Rue du Centre
   Port-au-Prince

HONDURAS

1. There is no national system. However, the Universidad Nacional Autónoma de Honduras Library System has been attending to loan requests on an informal basis. Its address is:

   Universidad Nacional Autónoma de Honduras
   Tegucigalpa—Honduras

HONG KONG

1. The system is based on the holdings of 4 major libraries: the University of Hong Kong Libraries, the Chinese University of Hong Kong Library, the Hong Kong Polytechnic Library and the Urban Services Department Library Headquarters. Each benefits from legal deposit.

2. a) Requests for loans should be sent to:

   Interlibrary Loans
   University of Hong Kong Libraries
   Pokfulam Road

   b) *Despatch of loans:* Air mail.

   c) *Return of loans:* Air mail.

3. a) Requests for photoduplicated material should be sent to:

    Address as in 2a above.

    b) *Despatch of photoduplicated material:* Air mail.

4. *Restrictions:* Rare books, journals, reference books and some books in special collections are not loaned. Some of the Hong Kong University theses are not available for photocopying without the author's permission.

5. *Request forms accepted:* IFLA or ALA forms preferred.

6. Charges

    a) *Loans:* Free.

    b) *Photoduplicated material:* HK$ 1.00.

    c) *35mm microfilm negative:* Not applicable.

    d) *35mm positive:* HK$ 0.50 (minimum HK$ 125.00) per frame.
        HK$ 410.00 per 100 foot reel.

    e) *Paper copy from microfilm:* HK$ 1.20 per copy.

    f) *Duplicate microfiche:* Not applicable.

    g) *Paper copy from microfiche:* HK$ 1.20 per copy.

7. Method of payment

    a) *Loans:* Not applicable.

    b) *Photoduplicated material:* Cheque or bank draft.

8. *Loan period:* One month.

9. *Renewal:* Not allowed.

HUNGARY

1. The system is centralised. Requests are routed by the National Centre according to union catalogues, the depository collections system and the special collections system.

2. a) Requests for loans should be sent to:

    National Széchényi Library
    International Loans
    H-1827 Budapest   **Telephone: 752–721**
                                                 Telex: 224226 BIBLN H
                                                 Fax: 568–731

    Each telex request should include the sender's full postal address and should be laid out exactly like a printed IFLA request form so that it can be used in place of a printed form.

    b) *Despatch of loans:* Registered post and air mail outside Europe.

    c) *Return of loans:* Registered post and air mail from outside Europe.

3. a) Requests for photoduplicated material should be sent to:

    Address as in 2a above.

    b) *Despatch of photoduplicated material:* Air mail outside Europe.

4. *Restrictions:* Reference works, old and rare books, works of special value, manuscripts and periodicals are not usually lent, but photocopies or microfilms of the parts requested can be supplied.

5. *Request forms accepted:* IFLA forms preferred.

6. Charges

    a) *Loans:* Postal costs may be waived by mutual agreement.

    b) *Photoduplicated material:* Minimum charge US$2.00.

    c) *35mm microfilm negative:* US$0.30 per exposure

    d) *35mm positive:* US$0.30 per exposure

    e) *Paper copy from microfilm:* US$0.25 per page

    f) *Duplicate microfiche:* US$2.00

    g) *Paper copy from microfiche:* US$0.50 per copy

    These prices include the cost of shipment by surface mail; air mail charges are invoiced separately

7. Method of payment

    a) *Loans:* Not applicable.

    b) *Photoduplicated material:* Invoices should be paid by International Reply coupons, although for payment of larger amounts cheques will be accepted.

8. *Loan period:* One month from date of receipt.

9. *Renewal:* Allowed but should be requested before the expiry of the current loan period.

10. *Additional information:* The National Széchényi Library stock is used for making photocopies and microfilms only.

ICELAND

1. The system is based on the collection of the library of the University of Iceland, Reykjavik, with a backup provided by a number of research and specialised libraries.

2. a) Requests for loans should be sent to:

        Háskólabókasafn
        University Library
        ÍS-101 Reykjavik

        Telephone: 354–1–694300
        Telex: 94016953 LIBR G
        Telefax: 354–1–21331

    b) *Despatch of loans:* Air mail.

    c) *Return of loans:* Air mail.

3. a) Requests for photoduplicated material should be sent to:

        Address as in 2a above.

    b) *Despatch of photoduplicated material:* Air mail.

4. *Restrictions:* No significant restrictions apply.

5. *Request forms accepted:* Any.

6. Charges

    a) *Loans:* Free.

    b) *Photoduplicated material:* No charge made for small orders; otherwise, 10 Kr per page.

    c) *35mm microfilm negative:*

    d) *35mm positive:*

    e) *Paper copy from microfilm:*   No information given.

    f) *Duplicate microfiche:*

    g) *Paper copy from microfiche:*

7. Method of payment

    a) *Loans:* Not applicable.

    b) *Photoduplicated material:* Where applicable, an invoice is supplied with the material.

8. *Loan period:* One month from date of receipt.

9. *Renewal:* Granted on request unless the item is required by another user.

10. *Additional information:* Requests for Islandica (material published in Iceland or otherwise relating to things Islandic) unavailable from the University Library will be forwarded to the appropriate library or research institute.

INDIA

1. There is no national system. The National Library, Calcutta, has a restricted loan service—restricted to certain categories of its own collection.

A. National Library

2.   a) Requests for loans should be sent to:

    The Librarian
    National Library
    Lending Section
    Calcutta—700 027   **Telephone: 45:5381**

    The Library telex number is CA-7935 but telex is not used for operating the international loans service, and requests should be sent on IFLA International Loan Request forms only.

    b) *Despatch of loans:* Surface mail unless otherwise specified.

    c) *Return of loans:* Surface mail unless otherwise specified.

3.   a) Requests for photoduplicated material should be sent to:

    Address as in 2a above.

    b) *Despatch of photoduplicated material:* Air mail.

4. *Restrictions:* Reference books, serials, pamphlets, Government documents, materials from gift collections or rare collections etc are not lent out. Photocopies of microfilms of articles can be supplied on request and on payment.

5. *Request forms accepted:* IFLA forms preferred but a request on the institutional letterhead may also be accepted.

6. Charges

    a) *Loans:* Postal costs only.

    b) *Photoduplicated material:* 50 paise per exposure.

    c) *35mm microfilm negative:* 80 paise per exposure. Minimum charge of RS. 15/-.

    d) *35mm positive:*

    e) *Paper copy from microfilm:* } No information given.

    f) *Duplicate microfiche:*

    g) *Paper copy from microfiche:* } Not applicable.

7. Method of payment

    a) *Loans:* Postage refunds on loans may be paid by International Reply coupons.

    b) *Photoduplicated material:* Payments in cash or cheque are accepted. Advance payment is sometimes required.

8. *Loan period:* One month from date of issue.

9. *Renewal:* One renewal may be granted on request.

10. *Additional information:* Material taken on loan from the National Library, Calcutta, should be returned only to the National Library, Calcutta.

B. INSDOC

2. There is no loan service.

3. a) Requests for photoduplicated material should be sent to;

    INSDOC
    14, Satsang Vihar Marg
    New Delhi 110067

    b) *Despatch of photoduplicated material:* Air mail.

4. *Restrictions:* None.

5. *Request forms accepted:* INSDOC order forms preferred.

6. Charges

    a) *Loans:* Not applicable.

    b) *Photoduplicated material:* RS 5/- per 5 pages or part thereof (for copies from indigenous sources).

    c) *35mm microfilm negative:*

    d) *35mm positive:*

    e) *Paper copy from microfilm:* } Price list available.

    f) *Duplicate microfiche:*

    g) *Paper copy from microfiche:*

7. Method of payment

    a) *Loans:* Not applicable.

    b) *Photoduplicated material:* Prepayment required.

8. *Loan period:*
9. *Renewal:*   } Not applicable.

INDONESIA*

1. The system is based on the Perpustakaan Nasional (National Library) and Pusat Dokumentasi Ilmiah Nasional (National Scientific Documentation Center).

A. PERPUSTAKAAN NASIONAL

2. a) Requests for loans should be sent to:

   Perpustakaan Nasional
   Il. Iman Bonjol No. 1
   Jakarta Pusat
   P.O. Box 3624   **Telephone: 021–342529**

   b) *Despatch of loans:* Air mail unless very expensive.

   c) *Return of loans:* Air mail not required.

3. a) Requests for photoduplicated material should be sent to:

   Address as in 2a above.

   b) *Despatch of photoduplicated material:* Only sent by air mail on request.

4. *Restrictions:* Originals of single or rare copies of works are not lent but photocopies may be made.

5. *Request forms accepted:* Any.

6. Charges

   a) *Loans:* Postage costs.

   b) *Photoduplicated material:* Rp 50.00 per page.

   c) *35mm microfilm negative:* Not applicable.

   d) *35mm positive:* Rp 50,000 per reel.

   e) *Paper copy from microfilm:* Not applicable.

   f) *Duplicate microfiche:* Rp 5,000 per envelope.

   g) *Paper copy from microfiche:* Not applicable.

7. Method of payment

   a) *Loans:*   } Payment should be made to the
   b) *Photoduplicated material:*   } Library's bank account.

8. *Loan period:* 3 months.

9. *Renewal:* Granted on application.

B. PUSAT DOKUMENTASI ILMIAH NASIONAL

2. There is no loan service.

3. a) Requests for photoduplicated material should be sent to:

Pusat Dokumentasi Ilmiah Nasional—LIPI
Jl. Gatot Soebroto
P.O. Box 3065/Jkt
Jakarta   **Telephone: 511063, 510719, 583465**
                                Telex: 45875 PDIN IA

    b) *Despatch of photoduplicated material:* Air mail.

4. *Restrictions:* None.

5. *Request forms accepted:* Any.

6. Charges

    a) *Loans:* Not applicable.

    b) *Photoduplicated material:* 1–10 pages.
                                Domestic request: US$ 0.30.
                                Foreign request: US$ 3.00.

    c) *35mm microfilm negative:* US$ 56.00 per reel.

    d) *35mm positive:* US$ 40.00 per reel.

    e) *Paper copy from microfilm:* US$ 0.10.

    f) *Duplicate microfiche:* US$ 0.40
                negative: US$ 1.30

    g) *Paper copy from microfiche:* US$ 0.10.

7. Method of payment

    a) *Loans:* Not applicable.

    b) *Photoduplicated material:* Bank draft.

8. *Loan period:* ⎫
                   ⎬ Not applicable.
9. *Renewal:* ⎭

IRAN

1. There is no national system.

2. There is no loan service.

3. a) Requests for photoduplicated material should be sent to:

National Library of Iran
30 Tir Street
Tehran 11364

Iranian Documentation Centre
P.O.Box 13185–1371
Tehran   **Telex: 214554 NCSR IR**
                                Fax: 662254

Central Library
Plan and Budget Organization
Bahavestan Square
Tehran 11365

    b) *Despatch of photoduplicated material:* No information given.

4. *Restrictions:* None.

5. *Request forms accepted:* IFLA forms.

6. Charges

    a) *Loans:* Not applicable.

    b) *Photoduplicated material:* $0.5 per page.

    c) *35mm microfilm negative:* $0.5 per frame.

    d) *35mm positive:*

    e) *Paper copy from microfilm:*

    f) *Duplicate microfiche:*   } No information given.

    g) *Paper copy from microfiche:*

7. Method of payment

    a) *Loans:* Not applicable.

    b) *Photoduplicated material:* Unesco coupons.

8. *Loan period:*

             } Not applicable.

9. *Renewal:*

IRAQ

1. There is no international lending system. The address of the national library is:

National Library
Bab Al-Muatham
P.O.Box 14340
Baghdad

IRELAND

1. The Library Council/An Chomhairle Leabharlanna operates the Regional Library Bureau for Ireland (including Northern Ireland). It publishes **Serial Holdings in Irish Libraries (SHIRL)** and in conjunction with the British Library produces a regional location list based on ISBNs. Interlibrary loan statistics and developments are published in the Annual Report of the Committee on Library Co-operation in Ireland. This Committee acts as an advisory body to the Library Council.

2. a) Requests for loans should be sent to:

    **The Library Council
    Interlending Department
    53/54, Upper Mount Street
    Dublin 2**

    **Telephone: 761167, 761963
    Telex: 93904 ICLS EI**

    b) *Despatch of loans:* Surface mail.

    c) *Return of loans:* Air mail not required.

3. a) Requests for photoduplicated material should be sent to:

    Address as in 2a above.

    b) *Despatch of photoduplicated material:* Surface mail.

4. *Restrictions:* May be imposed by the supplying library. Rare materials and serials are not normally lent, but photocopies are supplied where possible.

5. *Request forms accepted:* British Library Document Supply Centre request forms are preferred, but IFLA request forms are also acceptable.

6. Charges

    a) *Loans:* Postage costs only.

    b) *Photoduplicated material:*

    c) *35mm microfilm negative:*

    d) *35mm positive:*

    e) *Paper copy from microfilm:*   } No information given.

    f) *Duplicate microfiche:*

    g) *Paper copy from microfiche:*

7. Method of payment

    a) *Loans:*   } Invoices are sent to requesting libraries for recovery of postage

    b) *Photoduplicated material:*   } costs on loans and for the supply of photoduplicated material.

8. *Loan period:* 6 weeks.

9. *Renewal:* Granted at the discretion of the lending library.

ISRAEL

1. The system is based on thirteen academic and research libraries (members of the Standing Committee of National and University Libraries). This is supported by the **Union List of Serials in Israel Libraries.**

    The Jewish National and University Library, which has the oldest and largest collection in the country (approximately 2 million volumes) serves as a national lending centre.

    The library of the Technion—Israel Institute of Technology serves as a lending centre for material in the field of technology.

2. a) Requests for loans should be sent to:

    (i) Non-technical material

    Jewish National University Library
    P.O.Box 503
    Jerusalem   **Telephone: 02 585039**
                                                 Telex: 25367
                                                 Fax: 666804

    (ii) Technical material

    Technion—Israel Institute of Technology
    Technion City
    Haifa   **Telephone: 04–225111**
                                                 Telex: 46650

    b) *Despatch of loans:* Registered surface mail unless air mail is requested.

    c) *Return of loans:* Air mail not required.

3. a) Requests for photoduplicated material should be sent to:

    (i) Non-technical material:

    Address as in 2ai above.

    (ii) Technical material:

    Address as in 2aii above.

    b) *Despatch of photoduplicated material:* If light in weight, air mail. If heavy, by air mail only if requested.

4. *Restrictions:* Rare books and deposit copies are not lent. Serials in heavy use are not lent, but photocopies can be supplied.

5. *Request forms accepted:* Any.

6. Charges

    a) *Loans:* $5.

    b) *Photoduplicated material:* No information given.

    c) *35mm microfilm negative:* $0.35 per frame.

    d) *35mm positive:* 1 MTR positive = $1.25.

    e) *Paper copy from microfiche:* $0.20 per page.

    f) *Duplicate microfiche:* $1.00.

    g) *Paper copy from microfiche:* A4 = $0.50. B4 = $0.60. A3 = $0.70.

7. Method of payment

    a) *Loans:*
    b) *Photoduplicated material:*   } Money order of any kind.

8. *Loan period:* Four weeks.

9. *Renewal:* If the item is not required elsewhere, renewal for another four weeks is possible.

10. *Additional information:* Items should be sent direct to the supplying library.

ITALY

1. There is no national system and Italy has no national centre for interlending. However, international lending with the United Kingdom is centralised in the National Central Library of Rome. The main lending collections in the country are held:

    (i)   In state libraries under the Ministero per i beni culturali e ambientali, which are governed by a code dating from 1967, **Regolamento organico dele biblioteche pubbliche statali approvato con DPR, 5 settembre, 1967, No. 1501**. Two of these libraries, in Rome and Florence, are National Central Libraries with legal deposit status for the whole country.

    (ii) In university libraries under the Ministero della pubblica istruzione.

    (iii) In local libraries under regional or municipal governments.

    (iv) In other public and private special libraries with selected users, including the National Research Council Central Library, which benefits from legal deposit of all publications relating to science and technology.

    The main union catalogues in the country are as follows:

    Monographs:

    Primo catalogo collettivo delle biblioteche italiane. Roma, Istituto Centrale per il catalogo unico, 1962—
    (Retrospective Author Catalogue from the letter A to Barq, as well as the headings Dante Alighieri, Bibbia, Virgilio).

    Current Union Catalogue (Author cards) from 1958 to 1973 of Italian publications located in 34 State libraries, published on microfiche by the Istituto Centrale per il catalogo unico e per le informazioni bibliografiche.

    Bollettino delle opere moderne straniere acquistate dalle biblioteche pubbliche governative italiane. Roma, Biblioteca Nazionale Centrale, 1886—
    (Irregular, the last volume published covers the year 1984; 1985 is in proof sheet).

    Periodicals:

    Catalogo collettivo de periodici—Archivio ISRDS/CNR. Roma, ICCU, 1983 (microf.);
    Catalogo dei periodici delle Biblioteche Lombarde. Milano, 1964–1977 (vol. 7);
    Catalogo dei periodici correnti delle Biblioteche Lombarde. Milano, 1985– (vI: A-B/vIII: H-M);
    Catalogo delle pubblicazioni periodiche esistenti in varie biblioteche di Roma e Firenze. Citta del Vaticano, 1955;
    Elenco dei periodici correnti esistenti in varie biblioteche di Roma al lo gennaio 1964. A cura di Olga Pinto. Roma, 1967;
    Catalogo dei periodici esistenti in Biblioteche di Roma. A cura dell' Unione internazionale degli istituti di archeologia, storia e storia dell'arte in Roma. 3a edizione accresiuta. Roma 1985.
    Catalogo collettivo di periodici scientifici e tecnici. Roma: Universita degli studi e organi del CNR. A cura de Consiglio Nazionale delle Ricerche. Roma, 1976 (vol 2);
    Pubblicazioni periodiche esistenti nelle biblioteche pubbliche e negli Istituti universitari di Napoli (fino al 1950). Napoli, 1957 Supplemento aggiornato al 1965. Napoli, 1969.

    The Istituto Centrale per il catalogo unico delle biblioteche italiane e per le informazioni bibliografiche maintains 28 Retrospective Author catalogues on cards up to 1957 of State libraries, which are about to be published in microform, and the Union Serial Catalogue (cards) up to 1971, relating to 15 State libraries.

2. a) Requests for loans should be sent to:

        (i) From the UK

             Biblioteca Nazionale Centrale 'Vittorio Emanuele II'
             Roma
             Viale Castro Pretorio
             00185 Roma   **Telephone: 06/4989**

(ii) From other countries

Requests may be sent to the library that holds the item required or to one of the two National Central Libraries. The latter will then forward the requests to other libraries if necessary. The addresses of the National Central Libraries are:

Biblioteca Nazionale Centrale 'Vittorio Emanuele II'
Roma
Viale Castro Pretorio
00185 Roma   **Telephone: 06/4989**

Biblioteca Nazionale Centrale
Piazza Cavalleggeri 1
Firenze   **Telephone: 055/244441**

b) *Despatch of loans:* Air mail is not usually used.

c) *Return of loans:* Air mail not usually required.

3. a) Requests for photoduplicated material:

There is no national centre for photocopying. When no firm location is known, requests should be sent to one of the National Central Libraries (addresses as in 2a) or, for scientific material to the National Research Council Central Library:

Biblioteca Centrale del Consiglio Nazionale delle Richerche
Piazza Aldo Moro 7
Roma   **Telephone: 06/4993**
                             Fax: 06/4957241

b) *Despatch of photoduplicated material:* Air mail is not usually used except by the National Central Library, Florence.

4. *Restrictions*

General loan restrictions are given in the 1967 code, paragraphs 78–79. The National Central Library, Rome, will only lend duplicate copies of Italian publications printed after 1850, and does not lend periodicals.

General photoduplication restrictions are given in the 1967 code, paragraphs 73–74 and in a paper entitled **Normativa delle Riproduzione** by the director of the National Central Library, Rome, Dr A Maria Vichi Giorgetti.

5. *Request forms accepted:* The National Central Library of Rome accepts only IFLA request froms. The National Central Library of Florence will accept libraries' own forms but prefers IFLA forms.

6. Charges

a) *Loans:* Postage costs.

b) *Photoduplicated material:*

c) *35mm microfilm negative:*   Charges vary according to the institutions.

d) *35mm positive:*   The National Central Library, Florence, charges L 100 or

e) *Paper copy from microfiche:*   L 150 per page of photoduplicated material.

f) *Duplicate microfiche:*

g) *Paper copy from microfiche:*

At the National Central Library, Florence, microfilming is carried out by private photographic firms; duplicate microfiche and paper copy from microfiche are not available.

7. Method of payment

a) *Loans:* International Reply Coupons.

b) *Photoduplicated material:* International postal orders or International Reply Coupons (National Central Library, Florence). International Reply Coupons (National Central Library, Rome).

8. *Loan period:* One month.

9. *Renewal:* Not allowed (National Central Library, Rome).
National Central Library, Florence, allows renewal provided that the work is not requested by another library or by a student.

10. *Additional information:* A governmental commission has just revised the 1967 code about the lending service, according also to the realisation of the SBN (National Library Service), but the new rules do not yet have mandatory force.

The National Research Council Central Library and the Biblioteca de Archeologia et Storia dell'arte do not provide a loan service, only photocopies.

JAMAICA

1. Interlending is carried out by the focal points of the three major Information Network Systems.

    (i)   The Jamaica Library Service (JLS), the public library system, which lends material within its own network of libraries as well as overseas.

    (ii) The University of the West Indies (UWI) Mona, which participates in international interlending dealing with libraries overseas.

    (iii) The National Library of Jamaica (NLJ) which operates a National Referral Service whereby information is made available to libraries on the location of materials within the National Information System, including the JLS, the UWI and numerous special libraries within the public and private sectors.

    At present there is a **National Union List of Serials** but no union catalogue. The location of material is facilitated by detailed subject profiles of each library, maintained by the National Referral Service. The National Library will only supply photocopies of publications from its own collection. Once a referral is made, all transactions between lending and requesting libraries are made direct.

2. a) Requests for loans should be sent to:

    National Referral Service
    c/o National Library of Jamaica
    P.O.Box 823
    Kingston   **Telephone: 922–5533**
    Cables: NALIBJAM
    *Fax: 809–92–25567

    Interlibrary Loans
    Library
    University of the West Indies
    Mona, Kingston 7   **Telephone: (809) 927–0923**

    Jamaica Library Service HQ
    P.O.Box 58
    Kingston, Jamaica   **Telephone: (809) 63310**

    * Ask to have fax machine switched on if during normal working hours.

    b) *Despatch of loans:* Policies vary according to individual libraries. Generally loans will be sent by air mail if requested and if postage is refunded.

    c) *Return of loans:* Items sent by air mail should be returned by air mail.

3. a) Requests for photoduplicated material should be sent to:

Addresses as in 2a above.

   b) *Despatch of photoduplicated material:* Air mail. The University of the West Indies Library requires refund of postage for this service.

4. *Restrictions:* Serials and negative microfilm are not lent. University of the West Indies theses and West Indiana are lent only if duplicate copies are available. UWI theses may only be copied with the written permission of the author, to be obtained by the requestor. Maps, manuscripts, and prints in the National Library's collection are not normally photocopied.

5. *Request forms accepted:* The National Library prefers IFLA request forms; the University of the West Indies prefers IFLA or ALA request forms.

6. Charges

   a) *Loans:* Postal costs sometimes required.

   b) *Photoduplicated material:* J$ 0.70.

   c) *35mm microfilm negative:* J$ 15.00 per 10ft minimum.   National Library of Jamaica.

   d) *35mm positive:* J$ 21.00 per 10ft minimum.   Prices subject to change without notice

   e) *Paper copy from microfilm:* J$ 3.00 per exposure.

   f) *Duplicate microfiche:* J$ 5.50.

   g) *Paper copy from microfiche:* J$ 3.00 per exposure.

Microfilm prices for the UWI Library are available on request. Microfiche is not available from UWI.

7. Method of payment

   a) *Loans:*

   b) *Photoduplicated material:*   Cheque or money order.

8. *Loan period:* University of the West Indies Library: one month from date of receipt. Other libraries: 6 to 8 weeks for international requests, 3 to 4 weeks locally.

9. *Renewal:* Granted on application.

10. *Additional information:* Supplying and requesting libraries will normally deal directly with each other. The National Library prefers to be used as a library of last resort and only photoduplicated material is supplied.

JAPAN

1. There is no nationwide international lending system in Japan. The National Diet Library, the Japan Information Center of Science and Technology and several other libraries carry out international lending independently. The National Diet Library as the sole legal deposit library in Japan has a large collection of materials published in Japan since 1868 and provides a loan/photoduplication service of these holdings. The Japan Information Center of Science and Technology maintains an intensive collection of information in the field of science, technology and medicine thereby providing photoduplication services of requested materials that are available from JICST library holdings and from other cooperative libraries in Japan.

A.   National Diet Library

2.   a)   Requests for loans should be sent to:

   Library Cooperation Department
   National Diet Library
   Nagata-cho 1–10–1
   Chiyoda-ku, Toyko
   100 Japan

   b)   *Despatch of loans:* Registered air mail.

   c)   *Return of loans:* Air mail.

3.   a)   Requests for photoduplicated material should be sent to:

   Address as in 2a above.

   b)   *Despatch of photoduplicated material:* Air mail.

4.   *Restrictions:* Rare and precious materials, deteriorated old books, large-sized materials, reference books, pamphlets, serial publications, audio/visual records, microforms and doctoral dissertations cannot be lent.

5.   *Request forms accepted:* National Diet Library forms preferred.

6.   Charges

   a)   *Loans:* Postal costs.

   b)   *Photoduplicated material:* ¥35 per 257 x 364mm page.

   c)   *35mm microfilm negative:* First frame: ¥150
   Additional frame: ¥35.

   d)   *35mm positive:* (From the available negative film)
   First 30cm: ¥150
   Additional 30cm: ¥80.

   NB: When a part of a volume is requested to be microfilmed, a negative film will be provided. When the whole of a volume is to be microfilmed, only a positive copy can be provided, but the cost of a negative copy needed for the making of the positive is to be borne by the applicant in case the negative film for the volume is not held by the Library.

   e)   *Paper copy from microfilm:* By photography: 210 x 297mm: ¥100.
   By reader printer: 210 x 297mm: ¥50.

   f)   *Duplicate microfiche:* ¥190.

   g)   *Paper copy from microfiche:* 257 x 364mm: ¥60.

7.   Method of payment

   a)   *Loans:* Postal costs.

   b)   *Photoduplicated material:* Charges must be paid on a Japanese Yen base in principle by International Postal Money Order, Banker's Transfer (¥1,500 must be added per transfer) or Bank Draft payable in Tokyo (¥3,900 must be added per draft) upon receipt of the invoice which will be sent to the applicant after the forwarding of material.

8.   *Loan period:* One month or less, excluding transit time.

9.   *Renewal:* No information given.

B.   Japan Information Center of Science and Technology

2.   There is no loan service.

3. a) Requests for photoduplicated material should be sent to:

   Overseas Service Division
   JICST
   C.P.O. Box 1478
   Tokyo
   100–91 Japan   **Telephone: Tokyo (581) 6411**

   b) *Despatch of photoduplicated material:* Air mail.

4. *Restrictions:* ⎤
                  ⎬ No information given.
5. *Request forms accepted:* ⎦

6. Charges

   a) *Loans:* Not applicable.

   b) *Photoduplicated material:* Photocopy (including air mail fees):
      Minimum charge per request for up to 10 pages: US$ 13.50
      Each additional 10 pages: US$ 5.00

      Location search fee (Referral fee) per item: US$ 12.00

   c) *35mm microfilm negative:* ⎤

   d) *35mm positive:* ⎟

   e) *Paper copy from microfilm:* ⎬ No information given.

   f) *Duplicate microfiche:* ⎟

   g) *Paper copy from microfiche:* ⎦

7. Method of payment

   a) *Loans:* Not applicable.

   b) *Photoduplicated material:* Invoice.

8. *Loan period:* ⎤
                 ⎬ Not applicable.
9. *Renewal:* ⎦

JORDAN

1. There is no national system but bilateral agreements for cooperation exist between the major libraries in the country.

2. a) Requests for loans should be sent to:

   The University of Jordan Library
   Amman   **Telephone: (962–6) 843555**
                                             Telex: 21629 UNVJ Jo
                                             Fax: (962–6) 832318

   b) *Despatch of loans:* Surface mail.

   c) *Return of loans:* Air mail not required.

3. a) Requests for photoduplicated material should be sent to:

   Yarmouk University Library
   Irbid

   Jordan University of Science and Technology
   Irbid.

   b) *Despatch of photoduplicated material:* No information given.

4. *Restrictions:* Reference works, periodicals, rare books, theses and the Jordanian Collection are not available for loan.

5. *Request forms accepted:* Any.

6. Charges

   a) *Loans:* Free.

   b) *Photoduplicated material:* Up to 10 pages: US$ 5.0 Each extra page: US$ 0.1

   c) *35mm microfilm negative:* US$ 0.4 per unit.

   d) *35mm positive:* Not available.

   e) *Paper copy from microfilm:* US$ 0.5 per unit.

   f) *Duplicate microfiche:* US$ 0.4 per unit.

   g) *Paper copy from microfiche:* US$ 4 per unit.

7. Method of payment

   a) *Loans:* Not applicable.

   b) *Photoduplicated material:* Cheque payable to the University of Jordan Library.

8. *Loan period:* One month.

9. *Renewal:* Not allowed.

KENYA

1. There is no national system. However, some services (eg photocopies of sections of a periodical) are provided when possible. Once a policy has been formulated, then the system will become operational. Meanwhile each library operates its own service and may lend to an another library in Kenya but not outside the country.

2. There is no loan service.

3. a) Requests for photoduplicated material should be sent to:

   Individual libraries eg

   University of Nairobi
   Main Library
   P.O. Box 30197
   Nairobi

   b) *Despatch of photoduplicated material:* Varies according to individual libraries.

4. *Restrictions:* Varies according to individual libraries.

5.   *Request forms accepted:* Any (University of Nairobi).

6.   Charges

    a)   *Loans:* Not applicable.

    b)   *Photoduplicated material:* Ksh. 100 per page

    c)   *35mm microfilm negative:* ⎫

    d)   *35mm positive:* ⎬ Not available

    e)   *Paper copy from microfilm:* Ksh. 100 per page ⎫ University of Nairobi.

    f)   *Duplicate microfiche:* ⎫

    g)   *Paper copy from microfiche:* ⎬ Not available

7.   Method of payment

    a)   *Loans:* Not applicable.

    b)   *Photoduplicated material:* An invoice will be mailed with the material or before the material is despatched. Cheques are normally accepted.

8.   *Loan period:* ⎫

               ⎬ Not applicable.

9.   *Renewal:* ⎭

DEMOCRATIC PEOPLE'S REPUBLIC OF KOREA

1.   The Grand People's Study House DPRK, taking part in the international lending system organised under the auspices of the International Federation of Library Associations (IFLA), will lend its materials to libraries abroad.

2.   a)   Requests for loans should be sent to:

       The Grand People's Study House DPRK
       Division of International Loan
       P.O.Box 200. 207–610–0
       Pyongyang. Central District   **Telephone: 34066**

    b)   *Despatch of loans:* Usually registered air mail.

    c)   *Return of loans:* Registered mail.

3.   a)   Requests for photoduplicated material should be sent to:

       Address as in 2a above.

    b)   *Despatch of photoduplicated material:* Usually registered air mail.

4.   *Restrictions:* Material to be lent according to the present procedures will be those in the holdings of the Grand People's Study House DPRK, providing duplicate copies exist. Rare books and single copies of publications in great demand are not lent.

5.   *Request forms accepted:* IFLA forms or similar.

6. Charges

    a) *Loans:*

    b) *Photoduplicated material:*

    c) *35mm microfilm negative:*

    d) *35mm positive:*

    e) *Paper copy from microfilm:*

    f) *Duplicate microfiche:*   } No information given.

    g) *Paper copy from microfiche:*

7. Method of payment

    a) *Loans:*

    b) *Photoduplicated material:*

8. *Loan period:* One month or less, excluding transit time.

9. *Renewal:* No information given.

REPUBLIC OF KOREA

1. There is no central interlending and copying system. Requests for photoduplicates may be sent direct to individual libraries.

2.   a) Requests for loans should be sent to:

    The National Central Library
    San 60–1, Panpo-Dong
    Seocho-Gu
    Seoul 137–702

    Korea Institute for Economics and Technology
    P.O.Box 205, Cheongryang
    Seoul

    Interlibrary Loans Service
    Seoul National University Library
    San 56–1, Shillim-Dong, Kwanak-Gu
    Seoul 151–742

    National Assembly Library
    Yoido-Dong, Youngdungpo-Gu
    Seoul 150–703

  b) *Despatch of loans:* Air mail   } Seoul National University only.
  c) *Return of loans:* Air mail   The other three libraries do not run loan services.

3.   a) Requests for photoduplicated material should be sent to:

    Addresses as in 2a above.

  b) *Despatch of photoduplicated material:* Air mail.

4.   *Restrictions:* Subversive material and rare books are restricted (National Central Library).
     Subversive materials are restricted (KIET).
     Rare books and national treasures are restricted (Seoul National University Library).
     Subversive material and old books are restricted (National Assembly Library).

5.   *Request forms accepted:* Any, but Seoul National University Library prefers IFLA forms.

6.   Charges

     a)   *Loans:* Postal costs (Seoul National University Library only).

     b)   *Photoduplicated material:* W 100 per page (Seoul National University Library).

     c)   *35mm microfilm negative:*

     d)   *35mm positive:*

     e)   *Paper copy from microfilm:*   } No information given.

     f)   *Duplicate microfiche:*

     g)   *Paper copy from microfiche:* W 150 per page (Seoul National University Library).

7.   Method of payment

     a)   *Loans:* US$ cheque (Seoul National University Library only).

     b)   *Photoduplicated material:* US$ cheque (Seoul National University Library).
          Deposit Accounts (KIET).
          No information given for National Central Library or National Assembly Library.

8.   *Loan period:* One month

                                    } Seoul National University Library only.

9.   *Renewal:* Not allowed

KUWAIT*

2.   a)   Requests for loans should be sent to:

          Documentation Division
          Libraries Department
          Kuwait University   **Telex: 2616 KUNIVER KT**

     b)   *Despatch of loans:* Surface mail.

     c)   *Return of loans:* Surface mail.

3.   a)   Requests for photoduplicated material should be sent to:

          Address as in 2a above.

     b)   *Despatch of photoduplicated material:* Surface mail.

4.   *Restrictions:* Serials are not lent but photocopies may be supplied.

5.   *Request forms accepted:* Any.

6. Charges

    a) *Loans:* No information given.

    b) *Photoduplicated material:* 20 fils per page.

    c) *35mm microfilm negative:* 20 fils.

    d) *35mm positive:* 20 fils.

    e) *Paper copy from microfilm:* 21 × 29cm: 50 fils.
       29 × 42cm: 100 fils.

    f) *Duplicate microfiche:* 150 fils.

    g) *Paper copy from microfiche:* 21 × 29cm: 50 fils.
       29 × 42cm: 100 fils.

7. Method of payment

    a) *Loans:*

    b) *Photoduplicated material:* } Cheque or postal order.

8. *Loan period:* One month from date of receipt.

9. *Renewal:* No information given.

LESOTHO

1. There is no formal interlending system but local interlending is carried out. Lesotho National Library and the National University of Lesotho Library are registered members of the Interlibrary loan system based in Pretoria and the State Library acts as a clearing-house for Southern African libraries. Both libraries contribute to the union catalogue at the State Library.

2. a) Requests for loans should be sent to:

    Lesotho National Library Service
    P.O.Box 985
    Maseru—100   **Telephone: 323100 or 322592**

    b) *Despatch of loans:* Usually surface mail.

    c) *Return of loans:* Air mail only rarely required.

3. a) Requests for photoduplicated material should be sent to:

    National University Library
    P.O Roma 180   **Telephone: 340601**

    b) *Despatch of photoduplicated material:* Usually surface mail.

4. *Restrictions:* None.

5. *Request forms accepted:* State Library interlending forms.

6. Charges

    a) *Loans:* Free.

    b) *Photoduplicated material:* 20 cents per page.

c) *35mm microfilm negative:* ⎫
d) *35mm positive:* ⎬ Not applicable.

e) *Paper copy from microfilm:* 20 cents per page.

f) *Duplicate microfiche:* ⎫
g) *Paper copy from microfiche:* ⎬ Not applicable.

7. Method of payment

    a) *Loans:* Not applicable.

    b) *Photoduplicated material:* Crossed cheques and locally cash.

8. *Loan period:* One month.

9. *Renewal:* Allowed unless the item is in demand.

10. *Additional information:* Although the National Library does not participate in international lending/copying it accepts request forms from all over the world, which are sent to it directly. Satisfying requests is mostly by means of photocopying.

LIBYA*

2. a) Requests for loans should be sent to:

    Public Services Department
    Central Library
    P.O.Box 1308
    Garyounis University
    Benghazi

    b) *Despatch of loans:* Air mail.

    c) *Return of loans:* Air mail.

3. a) Requests for photoduplicated material should be sent to:

    Address as in 2a above.

    b) *Despatch of photoduplicated material:* Air mail.

4. *Restrictions:* Reference works, manuscripts and serials are not lent.

5. *Request forms accepted:* IFLA forms preferred.

6. Charges

    a) *Loans:*

    b) *Photoduplicated material:* ⎫

    c) *35mm microfilm negative:*

    d) *35mm positive:* ⎬ No information given.

    e) *Paper copy from microfilm:*

    f) *Duplicate microfiche:*

    g) *Paper copy from microfiche:* ⎭

7. Method of payment

a) *Loans:*

b) *Photoduplicated material:*

8. *Loan period:*

9. *Renewal:*

} No information given.

10. *Additional information:* Loans should be returned direct to the lending library.

LIECHTENSTEIN

1. The Liechtenstein Landesbibliothek takes part in the interlibrary loan system of Switzerland, based on a union catalogue. It also participates in its own right in international interlibrary lending. **The Liechtenstein Bibliography** (1960), published by the Landesbibliothek, provides information about the publishing output of Liechtenstein.

2. a) Requests for loans should be sent to:

   Liechtensteinische Landesbibliothek
   Postfach
   FL 9490 Vaduz   **Telephone: 075–6 63 43**

   b) *Despatch of loans:* Air mail.

   c) *Return of loans:* Air mail not required.

3. a) Requests for photoduplicated material should be sent to:

   Address as in 2a above.

   b) *Despatch of photoduplicated material:* Air mail.

4. *Restrictions:* Single copy items, published in Liechtenstein, are not available for loan; photocopies may be supplied.

5. *Request forms accepted:* IFLA forms.

6. Charges

   a) *Loans:* Postal costs.

   b) *Photoduplicated material:* 0.20 Swiss francs.

   c) *35mm microfilm negative:*

   d) *35mm positive:*

   } Not applicable.

   e) *Paper copy from microfilm:* 0.50 Swiss francs.

   f) *Duplicate microfiche:*

   g) *Paper copy from microfiche:*

   } Not applicable.

7. Method of payment

   a) *Loans:* International Reply Coupons.

   b) *Photoduplicated material:* Invoice.

8.	*Loan period:* 6 weeks.

9.	*Renewal:* Renewal of 4 weeks may be obtained on application.

LUXEMBOURG

1.	The system is based on the collections of the National Library (foreign publications and Luxemburgensia) which acts as the national centre for international lending and photocopying.

	The National Library does not, however, receive all the publications published in Luxembourg by the European Communities; requests for EC publications should therefore be sent to the appropriate EC-library.

2.	a)	Requests for loans should be sent to:

	Bibliothèque Nationale
	Service du Prêt International
	37, bd Roosevelt
	L—2450 Luxembourg　　　　　**Telephone: 26255**
	　　　　　　　　　　　　　　　Fax: 475672

	Requests for European Communities material should be sent to:

	Commission des Communautés Européennes
	Bibliothèque
	Bâtiment Jean Monnet
	Bureau Bo-lo
	L—2920 Luxembourg　　　　　**Telephone: 4301–3341**
	　　　　　　　　　　　　　　　Fax: Lux 436124 and 436125
	　　　　　　　　　　　　　　　Telex: 43013159 and 43012367

	Parlement Européen
	Bibliothèque
	Prêt inter-bibliothèques
	L—2929 Luxembourg　　　　　**Telephone: 4300–1**

	Cour de Justice Européenne
	Bibliothèque
	Prêt inter-bibliothèques
	L—2925 Luxembourg　　　　　**Telephone: 43884–1**

	Banque Européenne d'investissement
	Bibliothèque
	Prêt inter-bibliothèques
	L—2950 Luxembourg　　　**Telephone: 4379–6012 and 4379–6008**

	b)	*Despatch of loans:* BNL uses air mail overseas (and elsewhere on request). The other libraries use registered surface mail.

	c)	*Return of loans:* Air mail is preferred from overseas.

3.	a)	Requests for photoduplicated material should be sent to:

	Addresses as in 2a above.

	b)	*Despatch of photoduplicated material:* BNL uses air mail overseas (and elsewhere on request). The other libraries use registered surface mail.

4.	*Restrictions:* BNL does not lend rare national material but copies can sometimes be supplied at cost or on loan.

5. *Request forms accepted:* IFLA forms preferred.

6. Charges

   a) *Loans:* Free.

   b) *Photoduplicated material:* Up to 20 sheets free.
   Extra sheets: 5 Belgian francs } BNL
   per sheet

   c) *35mm microfilm negative:* Cost estimates on request.

   d) *35mm positive:* Not applicable.

   e) *Paper copy from microfilm:* Cost estimates on request;
   6–10 Belgian francs per sheet.

   f) *Duplicate microfiche:* Not applicable.

   g) *Paper copy from microfiche:* Cost estimates on request;
   6–10 Belgian francs per sheet.

7. Method of payment

   a) *Loans:* Not applicable.

   b) *Photoduplicated material:* International money order.

8. *Loan period:* One month.

9. *Renewal:* One month on request.

MADAGASCAR

1. Interlibrary lending is carried out locally in response to letter requests. International lending is by letter or request form and, in this case, photocopies are made and the costs charged to the requesting library.

2. There is no loan service.

3. a) Requests for photoduplicated material should be sent to:

   Bibliothèque Nationale
   B.P 257
   Antananarivo 101   Telephone: 258–72
                                                   205–11

   Bibliothèque Universitaire
   B.P 908
   Antananarivo 101   Telephone: 241–14
                                                   211–03

   b) *Despatch of photoduplicated material:* Air mail.

4. *Restrictions:* Precious documents (very old, unique examples etc) are not lent.

5. *Request forms accepted:* Letters on official headed paper are accepted as well as request forms like IFLA's.

6. Charges

   a) *Loans:* Not applicable.

   b) *Photoduplicated material:* 200 FMG per page. Postage costs are paid by the despatching library.

   c) *35mm microfilm negative:*

   d) *35mm positive:*

   e) *Paper copy from microfilm:* } Not applicable.

   f) *Duplicate microfiche:*

   g) *Paper copy from microfiche:*

7. Method of payment

   a) *Loans:* Not applicable.

   b) *Photoduplicated material:* Credit transfer.

8. *Loan period:*
   } Not applicable.
9. *Renewal:*

MALAWI

1. Malawi does not possess a formal system for either national or international lending. Interlending takes place on an informal basis.

   The largest lending collection in the country, belonging to the University of Malawi at Chancellor College, contains about 190,000 volumes. Smaller collections exist at Polytechnic (49,000); Bunda College of Agriculture (28,000); and Kamuzu College of Nursing (14,000); which are the other constituent libraries of the University of Malawi library system.

   A union catalogue of all University of Malawi libraries' holdings is maintained at Chancellor College Library.

   The other collection of note is at the National Archives, P.O.Box 62, Zomba. As the only copyright library in the country their collection of materials relating to Malawi is the best available.

   As there is no formal lending system in Malawi, no national interlending guidelines exist.

2. a) Requests for loans should be sent to:

   University of Malawi Library
   Chancellor College
   P.O.Box 280
   Zomba

   b) *Despatch of loans:* Air mail.

   c) *Return of loans:* Air mail.

3. a) Requests for photoduplicated material should be sent to:

   Address as in 2a above.

   b) *Despatch of photoduplicated material:* Air mail.

4. *Restrictions:* Books which would be difficult to replace are excluded from loan.

5. *Request forms accepted:* Any.

6. Charges

    a) *Loans:*

    b) *Photoduplicated material:* } Not usually made.

    c) *35mm microfilm negative:*

    d) *35mm positive:*

    e) *Paper copy from microfilm:* } Not applicable.

    f) *Duplicate microfiche:*

    g) *Paper copy from microfiche:*

7. Method of payment

    a) *Loans:*

    b) *Photoduplicated material:* } Not applicable.

8. *Loan period:* Usually 1–2 months.

9. *Renewal:* Granted on request.

MALAYSIA

1. The system is based on the National Library's holdings and the holdings of other major libraries in the country. A Publication Delivery System guidebook has been published and may be obtained from the National Library.

2. a) Requests for loans should be sent to:

    Director General
    National Library of Malaysia
    Reference Division
    1st Floor
    Wisma Sachdev
    Jalan Raja Laut
    50572 Kuala Lumpur   **Telephone: 2923144, 2923270,**
                                            2923348, 2923491,
                                                2981391
                          Telex: 30092 NATLIB MA
                          Fax: (03) 2917436

    b) *Despatch of loans:* Second class air mail, unless otherwise requested.

    c) *Return of loans:* Air mail if requested.

3. a) Requests for photoduplicated material should be sent to:

    Address as in 2a above.

    b) *Despatch of photoduplicated material:* Air mail.

4. *Restrictions:* 'Malaysiana' items, not held in multiple copies, rare books, manuscripts, maps, microform materials and serials (including bound and unbound newspapers) are not lent. Photocopies and positive microfilms of these materials can be supplied at cost.

5. *Request forms accepted:* Any.

6. Charges

    a) *Loans:* Postal costs.

    b) *Photoduplicated material:* M$ 0.20.

    c) *35mm microfilm negative:* M$ 160.00.

    d) *35mm positive:* M$ 100.00

    e) *Paper copy from microfilm:* M$ 0.75.

    f) *Duplicate microfiche:* M$ 0.45.

    g) *Paper copy from microfiche:* No information given.

7. Method of payment

    a) *Loans:* ⎫
    b) *Photoduplicated material:* ⎬ Malaysian currency.

8. *Loan period:* Usually one month from date of receipt.

9. *Renewal:* Granted on request.

10. *Additional information:* Items must be returned immediately when requested and should be sent direct to the lending library.

MALDIVES

1. There is no national system. The address of the national library is:

    National Library
    Billoorijehige
    59 Majeedi Magu
    Galolhu
    Malé

MALTA

1. There is no formal interlending system and no national centre for national and international lending. There are no national guidelines.

2. a) Requests for loans should be sent to:

        Inter-library Loans Department
        University of Malta Library
        Msida

        Telephone: 333903/6
        Cables: UNIVERSITY-MALTA
        Telex: 407 HIEDUC MW
        Fax: 356–314306

    b) *Despatch of loans:* Air mail.

    c) *Return of loans:* Air mail.

3. a) Requests for photoduplicated material should be sent to:

   Address as in 2a.

   b) *Despatch of photoduplicated material:* Air mail.

4. *Restrictions:* Books and dissertations are lent provided that duplicate copies are held.

5. *Request forms accepted:* IFLA forms preferred.

6. Charges

   a) *Loans:* Postal and packing charges.

   b) *Photoduplicated material:* 2 Maltese cents per page.

   c) *35mm microfilm negative:* ⎱
   d) *35mm positive:* ⎰ Not applicable.

   e) *Paper copy from microfilm:* 2 Maltese cents per page plus postage.

   f) *Duplicate microfiche:* ⎱
   g) *Paper copy from microfiche:* ⎰ Not applicable.

7. Method of payment

   a) *Loans:* ⎱
   b) *Photoduplicated material:* ⎰ Bank draft or British postal or money order

8. *Loan period:* One month.

9. *Renewal:* Usually granted.

MAURITANIA

1. There is no national system. The address of the national library is:

   Bibliothèque Nationale
   BP 26
   Nouakchott

MAURITIUS*

1. The University Library provides interlending facilities to local libraries for all material in its stock, with certain exceptions. No union catalogue has been produced.

2. a) Requests for loans should be sent to:

   The Librarian
   Inter-Library Loans
   University of Mauritius
   Reduit   Telephone: 4–5420
                                 54–1041

b) *Despatch of loans:* Registered second class air mail, unless otherwise requested.

c) *Return of loans:* Air mail.

3. a) Requests for photoduplicated material should be sent to:

   Address as in 2a above.

   b) *Despatch of photoduplicated material:* Air mail.

4. *Restrictions:* Mauritiana may be lent if a duplicate copy exists. Rare books and single copies of publications in great demand are not lent. Photocopies of these may be supplied at cost.

5. *Request forms accepted:* Official letters on headed paper or standard international request forms eg IFLA.

6. Charges

   a) *Loans:* Postal costs may be charged (depends on postal rates and weight of items being sent).

   b) *Photoduplicated material:* 1 rupee per page (+ charge for packing and posting by air mail).

   c) *35mm microfilm negative:*

   d) *35mm positive:*   } Prices available on request.

   e) *Paper copy from microfilm:* RS 11 (excluding postage).

   f) *Duplicate microfiche:* Not applicable.

   g) *Paper copy from microfiche:* RS 10 (40 x 60cm).

7. Method of payment

   a) *Loans:*

   b) *Photoduplicated material:*   } No information given.

8. *Loan period:* 3 months.

9. *Renewal:* Renewals for up to 2 weeks only may be granted on request.

MEXICO

1. There is no national or international lending system. However, the National Library will supply photocopies.

2. There is no loan service.

3. a) Requests for photoduplicated material should be sent to:

   Biblioteca Nacional de México
   Centro Cultural Universitario
   Ciudad Universitaria
   Delegacion Coyoacan, 04510

   b) *Despatch of photoduplicated material:* Air mail.

4. *Restrictions:* Old material in poor condition may not be photocopied.

5. *Request forms accepted:* Any.

6. Charges

    a) *Loans:* Not applicable.

    b) *Photoduplicated material:* US$ 1.00 for 10 copies (from books).
                                   US$ 2.00 for periodical articles.

    c) *35mm microfilm negative:* US$ 40.00 (50 images).

    d) *35mm positive:* US$ 25.00 (50 images).

    e) *Paper copy from microfilm:*

    f) *Duplicate microfiche:*   }   No information given.

    g) *Paper copy from microfiche:*

7. Method of payment

    a) *Loans:* Not applicable.

    b) *Photoduplicated material:* Cheque or postal Giro.

8. *Loan period:*
                     }   Not applicable.

9. *Renewal:*

MICRONESIA

1. Interlibrary loans are handled by the Robert F Kennedy Memorial Library, University of Guam. Special collections include the Micronesian Area Research Center (MARC), University of Guam Theses Collection and the University of Guam Special Projects Collection. There is no union catalogue. Guidelines for Micronesia's interlibrary loan system are available from the Interlibrary Loan Department, Robert F Kennedy Memorial Library, University of Guam.

2.   a) Requests for loans should be sent to:

      Interlibrary Loan Department
      Robert F. Kennedy Memorial Library
      University of Guam Station
      Guam 96923

    b) *Despatch of loans:* Air mail.

    c) *Return of loans:* Air mail.

3.   a) Requests for photoduplicated material should be sent to:

      Address as in 2a above.

    b) *Despatch of photoduplicated material:* Air mail.

4. *Restrictions:* Most materials at MARC are not available for loan, only for photoduplication.

5. *Request forms accepted:* ALA or IFLA forms.

6. Charges

    a) *Loans:* Free.

    b) *Photoduplicated material:* 10 cents per page.

c) *35mm microfilm negative:* ⎫
d) *35mm positive:*) ⎬ Not applicable.

e) *Paper copy from microfilm:* 10 cents per page.

f) *Duplicate microfiche:* Not applicable.

g) *Paper copy from microfiche:* 15 cents per page.

7. Method of payment

a) *Loans:* Not applicable.

b) *Photoduplicated material:* United States currency.

8. *Loan period:* Three weeks from arrival of material.

9. *Renewal:* Renewal possible if material is not needed by a University of Guam patron.

MONTSERRAT

1. There is no national system and no national library.

MOROCCO*

1. The system is based on the stock of the Morocco Bibliothèque Générale, which specialises in works concerning Morocco and Islam, and has a collection of Arabic manuscripts. It is supported by other libraries and documentation organisations in Morocco.

2. a) Requests for loans should be sent to:

   Service du Prêt International
   Bibliothèque Générale et Archives du Maroc
   Avenue Moulay Cherif
   Rabat

   b) *Despatch of loans:* Registered letter post and surface mail.

   c) *Return of loans:* No information given.

3. a) Requests for photoduplicated material should be sent to:

   Address as in 2a above.

   b) *Despatch of photoduplicated material:* Registered letter post and surface mail.

4. *Restrictions:* Large books weighing more than 1 kilogram, manuscripts and periodicals are not lent. Photocopies are made of periodical articles where exact references have been given.

5. *Request forms accepted:* IFLA forms or letters.

6. Charges

    a) *Loans:* Postal costs.

    b) *Photoduplicated material:*

    c) *35mm microfilm negative:*

    d) *35mm positive:*
    $\left.\right\}$ No information given.
    e) *Paper copy from microfilm:*

    f) *Duplicate microfiche:*

    g) *Paper copy from microfiche:*

7. Method of payment

    a) *Loans:* International Reply Coupons according to the weight of the work and the value of the coupon. (Morocco buys coupons at 1 Moroccan DH but they are reimbursed at 70 Moroccan C). Calculations should be made on this basis.

    b) *Photoduplicated material:* International Reply Coupons or cheques made payable to 'M. le Régisseur' at the above address.

8. *Loan period:* One month from date of receipt. Certain exceptions can be made on special request.

9. *Renewal:* No information given.

NAMIBIA

1. There is no national system. The system of the Republic of South Africa is still used.

    The major lending collection consists of all the Dewey classes and an Africana collection with mainly Southwest Africa/Namibia as its focus.

2. a) Requests for loans should be sent to:

    Estorff Reference Library
    P/Bag 13186
    Windhoek
    9000   **Telephone: (061) 229251 x633/638**
                                                                 Fax: (061) 226153

    b) *Despatch of loans:* Air mail.

    c) *Return of loans:* Air mail.

3. a) Requests for photoduplicated material should be sent to:

    Address as in 2a above.

    b) *Despatch of photoduplicated material:* Air mail.

4. *Restrictions:* The Africana collection is not lent but photoduplication of wanted items is possible.

5. *Request forms accepted:* Any.

6. Charges

    a) *Loans:* Free.

    b) *Photoduplicated material:* 0.20 cents per page (A4 or A3).

c) *35mm microfilm negative:* ⎫
d) *35mm positive:* ⎭ Not available.

e) *Paper copy from microfilm:* No information given.

f) *Duplicate microfiche:* Not available.

g) *Paper copy from microfiche:* 50 cents.

7. Method of payment

   a) *Loans:* Not applicable.

   b) *Photoduplicated material:* Nationally: the coupon system as prescribed by the State Library (RSA). Internationally: cash/cheque.

8. *Loan period:* Nationally: 6 weeks. Internationally: 3 months.

9. *Renewal:* No information given.

NEPAL

1. There is no national system. The address of the national library is:

   Nepal National Library
   Harihar Bhawan
   Pulchowk
   Lalitpur

THE NETHERLANDS

1. The system is based on three union catalogues, reporting holdings (250,000) of 356 academic, public and special libraries across the country. Co-operation between these three union catalogues led in 1980 to the building up of an automated national catalogue (NCC), with online retrieval facilities and an automated system of handling interlibrary loan requests.

   The NCC/ILL system for monographs will be operational in 1990. This system is based on the Pica-database (3,500,000 titles).

   There is no central collection.

2. a) Requests for loans should be sent to:

   (i) Social Sciences and Humanities material:

   Koninklijke Bibliotheek
   Centrale Catalogi
   Postbus 90407
   2509 LK 's-Gravenhage   **Telephone: 070–3140911**
   Telex: 34402 kbgv nl
   Fax: +31/70–140450

(ii) Engineering and Technical Sciences material:

Bibliotheek Technische Universiteit Delft
Centrale Technische Catalogus
Postbus 98
2600 MG Delft   **Telephone: 015–788013**
                                      Telex: 38070 bitud nl
                                      Fax: +31/15159007

(iii) Agricultural Sciences material:

Landbouwuniversiteit
Bibliotheek
Postbus 9100
6700 HA Wageningen   **Telephone: 08370–84440**
                                      Telex: 45015 bluwg nl
                                      Fax: +31/8370–84761

(iv) Agricultural Sciences material in English:

Wageningen Agricultural University
Library
P.O.Box 9100
6700 HA Wageningen

(v) National lending system for all (250,000) periodicals in the Netherlands:

NCC (Nederlandse Centrale Catalogus)
p/a Koninklijke Bibliotheek
Postbus 90407
2509 LK Den Haag   **Telephone: 070–3140389**
                                      Fax: 070–3140365

(vi) Experimental national lending system for books in the Netherlands (15 participants): NCC—
Monografieen

PICA
Centrum voor Bibliotheekautomatisering
Postbus 876
2300 AW Leiden   **Telephone: 071–257257**
                                      Fax: 071–223119

b) *Despatch of loans:* Air mail except to Belgium and Luxembourg (Bibliotheek Technische Universiteit Delft). Other libraries: Surface mail.

c) *Return of loans:* Registered air mail required (Bibliotheek Technische Universiteit Delft). Other libraries: No specific requirements.

3. a) Requests for photoduplicated material should be sent to:

    Addresses as in 2a above.

    b) *Despatch of photoduplicated material:* Air mail except to Belgium and Luxembourg (Bibliotheek Technische Universiteit Delft). Other libraries: Surface mail.

4. *Restrictions:* Rare books, manuscripts, reference materials, journals or heavy books are not lent but photocopies can be supplied on demand.

5. *Request forms accepted:* IFLA forms preferred.

6. Charges

    a) *Loans:*

    b) *Photoduplicated material:*   Charges vary.

    c) *35mm microfilm negative:*

d) *35mm positive:*

e) *Paper copy from microfilm:*

f) *Duplicate microfiche:* } Charges vary.

g) *Paper copy from microfiche:*

7. Method of payment

    a) *Loans:* } International money orders or

    b) *Photoduplicated material:* } International Reply Coupons.

8. *Loan period:* 8 weeks.

9. *Renewal:* Allowed unless the item is required elsewhere.

NETHERLANDS ANTILLES

1. There is no national system but requests will be dealt with. Each library has its own interlending system.

2.   a) Requests for loans should be sent to:

    Library University of the Netherlands Antilles
    P.O.Box 3059
    Curacao   **Telephone: 9–599–84422 Ex 110/111**
                                  Fax: 9–599–85465

    Philipsburg Jubilee Library
    P.O.Box #2
    St Maarten   **Telephone: (5995) 22970**
                                  Fax: (5995) 25805

    b) *Despatch of loans:* Air mail (Philipsburg Jubileee Library). Surface mail for heavy items; air mail for other items (Library University of the Netherlands Antilles).

    c) *Return of loans:* Air mail (Philipsburg Jubilee Library). Air mail except heavy items may be returned by surface mail (Library University of the Netherlands Antilles).

3.   a) Requests for photoduplicated material should be sent to:

    Addresses as in 2a above.

    b) *Despatch of photoduplicated material:* Air mail (Philipsburg Jubilee Library). Air mail except for very heavy items (Library University of the Netherlands Antilles).

4. *Restrictions:* Philipsburg Jubilee Library does not lend rare material. Library University of the Netherlands Antilles does not lend its Antillian collection.

5. *Request forms accepted:* Any.

6. Charges

    a) *Loans:* Free as yet (Philipsburg Jubilee Library). Library University of the Netherlands Antilles charges.

    b) *Photoduplicated material:* US$ 0.25 (Philipsburg Jubilee Library).
                         NAf 0.25 (Library University of the Netherlands Antilles).

c) *35mm microfilm negative:* ⎫
d) *35mm positive:* ⎬ Not applicable.

e) *Paper copy from microfilm:* US$ 0.25 (Philipsburg Jubilee Library).

f) *Duplicate microfiche:* ⎫
g) *Paper copy from microfiche:* ⎬ Not applicable.

7. Method of payment

   a) *Loans:* ⎫ Not yet established at Philipsburg Jubilee Library. No infor-
   b) *Photoduplicated material:* ⎬ mation given for Library University of the Netherlands Antilles.

8. *Loan period:* 2 weeks (Philipsburg Jubilee Library).
   2 months (Library University of the Netherlands Antilles).

9. *Renewal:* Allowed unless item is required elsewhere.

10. *Additional information:* If Library University of the Netherlands Antilles does not hold the required item, the request will be passed on to other libraries.

NEW ZEALAND

1. The national lending system is based on the New Zealand Bibliographic Network (NZBN) which was established in 1982 and maintains a comprehensive national holdings database of monographs from that date. As not all libraries have added their holdings retrospectively to NZBN, for earlier monograph holdings the system also depends on the Union Catalogue on microfiche which was filmed in 1986. Holdings of serials are recorded on FIND which is a database on KIWINET. Both NZBN and KIWINET are maintained by the National Library of New Zealand. National guidelines for interloan are laid down in the **Interloan Handbook 1986**. (Wellington: New Zealand Library Association, 1986).

2. a) Unless holdings in New Zealand libraries are known from NZBN, NZUC or FIND, loan requests should be sent to:

   Interloans Unit
   Reference and Interloan Services
   National Library of New Zealand
   P.O.Box 3342
   Wellington

   Telephone: (04) 743–000
   Telex: NATLIB NZ30076
   Fax: (04) 858–077 or (04) 743035
   Electronic mail: SZN006 (6401:SZN006)

   b) *Despatch of loans:* Air mail.

   c) *Return of loans:* Air mail.

3. a) Unless holdings in New Zealand libraries are known from NZBN, NZUC or FIND, requests for photoduplicated material should be sent to:

   Address as in 2a above.

   b) *Despatch of photoduplicated material:* Air mail.

4. *Restrictions:* These vary from library to library within New Zealand. The National Library of New Zealand may withold rare New Zealand books and will not normally lend whole issues of serials.

5. *Request forms accepted:* IFLA forms preferred.

6. Charges

Charges vary from library to library within New Zealand. The National Library of New Zealand's practices are given below.

a) *Loans:*

b) *Photoduplicated material:* } Free.

c) *35mm microfilm negative:*

d) *35mm positive:* } $25–$37 depending on the number of frames.

e) *Paper copy from microfilm:*

f) *Duplicate microfiche:* } Free.

g) *Paper copy from microfiche:* No charge for a printout of a proportion of a fiche. Complete paper printouts are provided only if copyright allows and if the requesting library does not have fiche-reading facilities.

7. Method of payment

a) *Loans:*

b) *Photoduplicated material:* } Not applicable.

8. *Loan period:* 2 months.

9. *Renewal:* Not allowed.

10. *Additional information:* The National Library of New Zealand endeavours to satisfy all requests it receives. Only when requested items are not held are requests sent on to other holding libraries within New Zealand. When this happens loans should be returned direct to the lending library, not back to the National Library of New Zealand.

NICARAGUA

1. There is no national system. The address of the national library is:

Biblioteca Nacional
Apdo 101
Managua

NIGERIA

1. The system is based on the National Library which acts as the National Clearing House for the receipt and processing of requests. Material is sent/returned direct between libraries.

2. a) Requests for loans should be sent to:

   Readers Services Division
   Inter-Library Lending
   4 Wesley Street
   P.M.B 12626
   Lagos

   Telephone: 630053, 634704
   Telex: 21746
   (answer back NET TDS NG)

   b) *Despatch of loans:* Air mail.

   c) *Return of loans:* Air mail not required.

3. a) Requests for photoduplicated material should be sent to:

   Address as in 2a above.

   b) *Despatch of photoduplicated material:* Air mail.

4. *Restrictions:* None.

5. *Request forms accepted:* IFLA forms preferred.

6. Charges

   a) *Loans:* Postal costs.

   b) *Photoduplicated material:* 50k per page.

   c) *35mm microfilm negative:*

   d) *35mm positive:*

   e) *Paper copy from microfilm:* } Not applicable.

   f) *Duplicate microfiche:*

   g) *Paper copy from microfiche:*

7. Method of payment

   a) *Loans:*

   b) *Photoduplicated material:* } Invoices are sent with the items.

8. *Loan period:* 1 month for local requests.
   2–3 months for international requests.

9. *Renewal:* Allowed on request (2 weeks locally and 1 month for international requests).

NORWAY

1. The system is based on seven subject specialised libraries, plus the Royal University Library in Oslo which also functions as the National Library. The National Library Branch at Mo i Rana became operative in July 1990. Its main task is the receipt and distribution of Norwegian publications received under legal deposit. One of the copies is available for loan.

    A Guide to interlibrary lending (in Norwegian) can be obtained from Norsk Samkatalog, Royal University Library in Oslo.

    Different conditions apply at each library and requestors should obtain specific information direct from the library concerned.

2. a) Requests for loans should be sent directly to the libraries listed below, depending on the subject/discipline.

    i)   General:

    Royal University Library in Oslo
    Drammensv. 42
    Oslo 2   Telephone: (02) 55 36 30
                                            Telex: 76078 ub n
                                            Fax: (02) 43 44 97

    NBR i Rana
    PB 278
    8601 Mo   Telephone: 087 21 111
                                            Fax: 087 55460

    ii) Medicine:

    University of Oslo Library
    Faculty of Medicine Library
    PB 1113 Blindern
    0317 Oslo 3   Telephone: (02) 45 40 33
                                            Telex: 19 792 umed n
                                            Fax: (02) 45 41 31

    iii) Technology:

    The Technical University Library of Norway
    Hogskolerigen 1
    7034 Trondheim   Telephone: (07) 59 51 00
                                            Telex: 55 186 nthb n
                                            Fax: (07) 59 51 03

    iv) Natural Sciences:

    University of Oslo Library
    Faculty of Mathematics and Natural Sciences Library
    PB 1063 Blindern
    0316 Oslo 3   Telephone: (02) 45 61 51
                                            Telex: 76639 ubmnf n
                                            Fax: (02) 69 24 99

    v)   Economics:

    Norwegian School of Economics and Business Administration
    The Library
    Hellev. 30
    5035 Bergen-Sandviken   Telephone: (05) 95 94 11
                                            Telex: 40642 nhh n
                                            Fax: (05) 25 83 83

vi) Agriculture:

The Norwegian College of Agriculture
The Library
PB 12
1432 Ås-NLH   **Telephone: (09) 94 83 02**
                                        Telex: 17125 nlhb n
                                        Fax: (09) 94 83 13

vii) Veterinary Medicine:

The Norwegian College of Veterinary Medicine
The Library
PB 8146 Dep
0033 Oslo 1   **Telephone: (02) 69 62 16**
                                          Fax: (02) 56 57 04

viii) Sports:

The Norwegian College of Physical Education and Sport
The Library
Sognsv. 220
PB 40 Kringsjå
0807 Oslo 8   **Telephone: (02) 23 46 85**
                                        Fax: 02 23 42 20

For extensive collection of Polar literature, contact:

The University Library
Tromsø
PB 678
9001 Tromsø   **Telephone: (083) 44 000**
                                        Telex: 64427 ubhov n
                                        Fax: (083) 80836

b) *Despatch of loans:*
c) *Return of loans:* } Practice varies.

3. a) Requests for photoduplicated material should be sent to:
   Addresses as in 2a above.

   b) *Despatch of photoduplicated material:* Varies.

4. *Restrictions:* Varies.

5. *Request forms accepted:* IFLA forms.

6. Charges
   a) *Loans:* Varies, but all libraries charge postal costs.

   b) *Photoduplicated material:* Mostly, Nkr 2,—per page.

   c) *35mm microfilm negative:*
   d) *35mm positive:*
   e) *Paper copy from microfilm:* } Charges vary.
   f) *Duplicate microfiche:*
   g) *Paper copy from microfiche:*

7. Method of payment

a) *Loans:*

b) *Photoduplicated material:* } Varies.

8. *Loan period:* Usually 4 weeks.

9. *Renewal:* Allowed unless item is required by another user.

PAKISTAN*

1. The National Library of Pakistan is currently being established in Islamabad, where a permanent building is under construction. The National Library is at present able to accept only a limited number of international requests for loans and photocopies which are provided free of charge.

The Pakistan Scientific and Technological Information Centre (PASTIC) deals with international lending and photocopying of scientific and technical material.

2. a) Requests for loans should be sent to:

Government of Pakistan
Department of Libraries
House No. 555 St. 83
G. 6/4
Islamabad   **Telephone: 22449**

PASTIC
Quaid-i-Azam University Campus
Islamabad

b) *Despatch of loans:*

c) *Return of loans:* } No information given.

3. a) Requests for photoduplicated material should be sent to:

Addresses as in 2a above.

b) *Despatch of photoduplicated material:* No information given.

4–9. No further information given.

PAPUA NEW GUINEA

1. National and international lending systems are in operation. The national lending system is not as busy as the international lending system. It lacks a proper union catalogue for monographs and proper guidelines. There is, however, a **National Union [Catalogue] of Serials held in PNG Libraries**.

2. a) Requests for loans should be sent to:

    Matheson Library
    University of Technology PNG
    Private Mail Bag Service
    Lae

    Goroka Teachers' College Library
    P.O.Box 1078
    Goroka

    Michael Somare Library
    The University of Papua New Guinea
    P.O.Box 319
    University Post Office

    National Library Service
    P.O.B 5770
    Boroko

    b) *Despatch of loans:* Air mail.

    c) *Return of loans:* Air mail.

3. a) Requests for photoduplicated material should be sent to:

    Addresses as in 2a above.

    b) *Despatch of photoduplicated material:* Air mail.

4. *Restrictions:* The maximum book loan is six. Theses may not be loaned or photoduplicated.

5. *Request forms accepted:* IFLA forms.

6. Charges

    a) *Loans:* Postal costs are required only when excessive.

    b) *Photoduplicated material:* Up to 20 pages free.
        Additional pages: 10 toea each.

    c) *35mm microfilm negative:* ⎫
                                   ⎬ Not applicable.
    d) *35mm positive:* ⎭

    e) *Paper copy from microfilm:* 10 toea.

    f) *Duplicate microfiche:* Not applicable.

    g) *Paper copy from microfiche:* 20 toea.

7. Method of payment

    a) *Loans:* Voucher ($6 per book loaned).

    b) *Photoduplicated material:* Voucher/cheque.

8. *Loan period:* 4 weeks.

9. *Renewal:* Granted unless the item is requested by another reader and may be done by telephone or by letter.

10. *Additional information:* The National Library in Papua New Guinea participates in international lending/copying on behalf of smaller libraries and, in some cases, individual requesters. All materials should be sent/returned through the National Library.

Institutional libraries eg University of Papua New Guinea, University of Technology and Goroka Teachers' College participate themselves.

Overseas libraries wishing to request items should direct requests to any of these bigger libraries.

PERU

1. There has been a national and international photocopy and microfilm service since 1960. Since 1986, however, the programme has expanded due to donations of equipment and the aim of the General Department of Conservation, Restoration and Reprographics is to provide a supply service of microfilm, photocopies and occasionally photographic copies in response to internal and international requests.

   Requests must contain precise bibliographic details and should be sent by air mail. Payment must be made before items are supplied.

2. a) Requests for loans should be sent to:

   Biblioteca Nacional del Peru
   Avenida Abancay Cuarta Cuadra
   Apartado 2335
   Lima   **Telephone: 28–7690**

   b) *Despatch of loans:* Air mail.

   c) *Return of loans:* Air mail.

3. a) Requests for photoduplicated material should be sent to:

   Address as in 2a above.

   b) *Despatch of photoduplicated material:* Air mail.

4. *Restrictions:* None.

5. *Request forms accepted:* IFLA forms.

6. Charges

   a) *Loans:* Charges are made. There is no exchange programme as yet.

   b) *Photoduplicated material:* 1–10 photocopies: $10.00.
   These contain 1 or 2 pages depending on format.

   c) *35mm microfilm negative:* ⎫
   d) *35mm positive:* ⎬ Varies.

   e) *Paper copy from microfilm:* $0.50.

   f) *Duplicate microfiche:* Varies.

   g) *Paper copy from microfiche:* A4: $1.00. A3: $1.50.

7. Method of payment

a) *Loans:*

b) *Photoduplicated material:*

An invoice in dollars is sent by registered air mail. Cheques should be made out to the Biblioteca Nacional del Peru-Tesorería. The item is supplied after payment is received. The cost of registered air mail is from $6.00 depending on weight.

8. *Loan period:* 1–2 months.

9. *Renewal:* Allowable.

THE PHILIPPINES

1. The National Library of the Philippines provides interlending facilities both at the national and international level. The lending system was called the National Libraries and Documentation Center of Southeast Asia Consortium (NLDC-SEA Consortium). It was established in 1979 consisting of the following members: Indonesian National Scientific Documentation Centre (PDIN), National Library of Malaysia, National Library of the Philippines, National Library of Singapore and National Library of Thailand.

In 1989, the Consortium was further strengthened; Brunei became a new member. It is now called Library Networking and Interchange of Materials Among ASEAN Countries, the objectives of which are the following:

a) To develop an inter-library system for the national libraries of Southeast Asia.

b) To provide access to all library materials, except classified items, emanating from countries of the Consortium at a reasonable cost and within reasonable time.

The **Philippine National Union Catalogue** (P.N. UNICAT) is still being developed and a database being built up.

2. a) Requests for loans should be sent to:

CLO Philippines
NLDC-SEA Consortium
Bibliography Division
The National Library of the Philippines
T.M. Kalaw St
Ermita
Manila 1000　　　　　　　　　　**Telephone: 50–10–11**
　　　　　　　　　　　　　　　　　Telex: 40726 NALIB PM

b) *Despatch of loans:* Surface, sea or air mail as requested.

c) *Return of loans:* Air mail not required.

3. a) Requests for photoduplicated material should be sent to:

Address as in 2a above.

b) *Despatch of photoduplicated material:* Air mail if the requesting party is willing to pay the postal charges.

4. *Restrictions:* Rare books and single copies of publications in great demand are not lent. However, photocopies of these may be supplied at cost.

5. *Request forms accepted:* IFLA forms and other official requests.

6. Charges

   a) *Loans:* Postal costs plus P1.00 per page if the item exceeds 10 pages.

   b) *Photoduplicated material:* P1.00 per page plus postal costs.

   c) *35mm microfilm negative:* Price available on request.

   d) *35mm positive:*

   e) *Paper copy from microfilm:*

   f) *Duplicate microfiche:* } Prices are available on request.

   g) *Paper copy from microfiche:*

7. Method of payment

   a) *Loans:*

   b) *Photoduplicated material:* } Cheques should be made payable to the National Library of the Philippines. Account No. BS/A No. 220–560034–8.

8. *Loan period:* Maximum of six months.

9. *Renewal:* Allowed on request for one month depending upon the demands of the material.

POLAND

1. There is no centralised system. The National Library acts as a centre only for requests received from or sent to the United Kingdom. For other countries loan requests are sent as well as received and dealt with directly by individual libraries. Requests may be made direct to a library specialising in the subject concerned. If a library is unable to supply a document from its own stock, it will forward requests to other libraries in Poland. The National Library maintains union catalogues and bibliographies with library codes and can therefore ascertain locations for items requested.

   National guidelines: Disposition of the Minister of Culture and Art of March 25, 1980 concerning the regulations for the interlibrary loans published in **'Monitor Polski' 1980, no 12, poz. 54.**

2. a) Requests for loans should be sent to:

   Biblioteka Narodowa
   International Loans
   Al. Niepodleglosci 213
   02–555 Warszawa   **Telex: 816761 bn pl**

   b) *Despatch of loans:* Europe: registered surface mail.
      Overseas: registered air mail.

   c) *Return of loans* Europe: Surface mail.
      Overseas: Air mail.

3. a) *Requests for photoduplicated material should be sent to:*

   Address as in 2a above.

   b) *Despatch of photoduplicated material:* Air mail only outside Europe.

4. *Restrictions:* Manuscripts, newspapers and unbound periodicals, rare and valuable books are not available for loan. Photocopies or microfilms of newspapers and unbound periodicals can be supplied.

5. *Request forms accepted:* IFLA forms preferred.

6. Charges

    a) *Loans:* Free. Postage costs are recovered on a reciprocal basis.

    b) *Photoduplicated material:* Up to 10 pages free.
        Additional pages: $0.12 per A4 page.

    c) *35mm microfilm negative:* $0.15 for 1 frame.

    d) *35mm positive:* $1.00 for one running metre.

    e) *Paper copy from microfilm:* $0.30 (A4 size).
        $0.60 (A3 size).

    f) *Duplicate microfiche:* Not applicable.

    g) *Paper copy from microfiche:* $0.15.

7. Method of payment

    a) *Loans:* Refund of postage is preferred in International Reply Coupons.

    b) *Photoduplicated material:* Invoices are issued. Payment is by International Reply Coupons or remittance payable to the Biblioteka Narodowa bank account.

8. *Loan period:* One month from date of receipt.

9. *Renewal:* Allowed on request.

10. *Additional information:* All material should be sent/returned directly to the library concerned.

PORTUGAL

1. There is no national lending system in operation. The National Library as well as the Central Library of the University of Coimbra are working at its implementation but it is not operational yet.

    Meanwhile, university libraries mainly the Library of the University of Coimbra provide interloan services but they are not organised in a system.

    The Centro de Documentação Científica et Técnica (CDCT) of the Instituto Nacional de Investigação Cientifica (INIC) is responsible for the production and management of the union list of periodicals existing in Portuguese libraries which is now accessible on-line via the public data transmission network. The List covers 25,000 titles held at 400 libraries. The Centro is able to accept requests for photoduplicated material from abroad and circulate them to other libraries. Loans are not normally supplied.

2. There is no loan service.

3. a) Requests for photoduplicated material should be sent to:

        INIC/CDCT
        Av. Prof. Gama Pinto 2
        1699 Lisboa Codex
        Telephone: +351 1 731300 or 731350
        Telex: 62593 IIFM P
        Fax: +351 1 765622

    b) *Despatch of photoduplicated material:* Air mail.

4. *Restrictions:* There are some restrictions on the photoduplication of old material due to preservation reasons.

5. *Request forms accepted:* IFLA forms.

6. Charges

    a) *Loans:* Not applicable.

    b) *Photoduplicated material:* The same charges as the British Library Document Supply Centre are applied.

    c) *35mm microfilm negative:*

    d) *35mm positive:*

    e) *Paper copy from microfilm:* } Not applicable.

    f) *Duplicate microfiche:*

    g) *Paper copy from microfiche:*

7. Method of payment

    a) *Loans:* Not applicable.

    b) *Photoduplicated material:* Cheque or bank transfer.

8. *Loan period:*

9. *Renewal:* } Not applicable.

PUERTO RICO

1. There is no national system.

2.   a) Requests for loans should be sent to:

    Préstamos Interbibliotecarios
    Sistema de Bibliotecas
    Apartado Postal 21371
    Río Piedras, P.R. 00931–1371   **Telephone: (809) 764–0000 Ext 3343**

    b) *Despatch of loans:* Air mail; postal library rate.

    c) *Return of loans:* Air mail not required.

3.   a) Requests for photoduplicated material should be sent to:

    Address as in 2a above.

    b) *Despatch of photoduplicated material:* Air mail.

4. *Restrictions:* Theses, periodicals, rare books, reference books, newspapers and unique copies of materials not available in the book market; manuscripts, posters, realia, art works, and records are not loaned. No photocopies are made of theses and dissertations from the University of Puerto Rico.

5. *Request forms accepted:* IFLA, ALA and OCLC forms.

6. Charges

    a) *Loans:* Free.

    b) *Photoduplicated material:* $0.10 per page.

c) *35mm microfilm negative:* $0.35 per foot.

d) *35mm positive:* $0.35 per foot.

e) *Paper copy from microfilm:* $0.10 per page.

f) *Duplicate microfiche:* Not applicable.

g) *Paper copy from microfiche:* $0.10 per page.

7. Method of payment

a) *Loans:* Not applicable.

b) *Photoduplicated material:* Cheque or money order payable to the University of Puerto Rico.

8. *Loan period:* One month.

9. *Renewal:* Allowed unless the material has been requested by another user.

QATAR

1. The National Library provides interlending facilities for all printed materials in its stock to six public library branches. A union catalogue has been produced. There is no system for international lending. The address of the national library is:

National Library
PO Box 205
Doha   **Telephone: 42 9955**
                                            Telex: 47 43 QANALI

ROMANIA

1. The system is based on the central collection of the Central State Library supported by union catalogues and a few large libraries.

2. a) Requests for loans should be sent to:

Biblioteca Centrală de Stat
Centrul Naţional de Schimb
Str. Ion Ghica, 4
Bucureşti, 70018   **Telephone: 14 24 34**

b) *Despatch of loans:* Air and surface mail.

c) *Return of loans:* Air mail preferred.

3. a) Requests for photoduplicated material should be sent to:

Address as in 2a above.

Biblioteca Academiei Romane
Calea Victoriei, 125
Bucureşti, 71102   **Telephone: 50 30 43**

Biblioteca Centrala Universitara
Str. Onesti, 1
Bucureşti, 70119

Biblioteca Centrala Universitara Cluj-Napoca
Str. Clinicilor, 2
Cluj-Napoca, 3400   Telephone: 17 092

Biblioteca Centrala Universitara 'M. Eminescu'
Str. Păcurari, 4
IASI, 6600   Telephone: 40 709

    b)   *Despatch of photoduplicated material:* Air and surface mail.

4.   *Restrictions:* Rare books are not loaned.

5.   *Request forms accepted:* IFLA forms.

6.   Charges

    a)   *Loans:* Postal costs.

    b)   *Photoduplicated material:* British Library Document Supply Centre system.

    c)   *35mm microfilm negative:*
                      } No information given.
    d)   *35mm positive:*

    e)   *Paper copy from microfilm:*
    f)   *Duplicate microfiche:*   } Not applicable.
    g)   *Paper copy from microfiche:*

7.   Method of payment

    a)   *Loans:*
                      } International Reply Coupons.
    b)   *Photoduplicated material:*

8.   *Loan period:* One month from date of receipt.

9.   *Renewal:* Allowed.

RWANDA

1.   There is no general national or international inter-lending system in operation.

ST LUCIA

1.   There is no national system. Individual libraries have their own arrangements.

ST VINCENT AND THE GRENADINES

1. The Department of Libraries, Archives and Documentation Services provides interlending services at both national and regional levels. Some material is not for loan. No union catalogue has yet been produced.

2. a) Requests for loans should be sent to:

    The Director
    Department of Libraries, Archives and Documentation Services
    c/o Public Library
    Granby Street
    Kingstown
    St Vincent and the Grenadines
    West Indies

    The Librarian
    Documentation Centre
    Ministerial Building
    Halifax Street
    Kingstown
    St Vincent and the Grenadines
    West Indies   **Telex: 7531 FOREIGN VQ**
    Fax: 45–72943

    b) *Despatch of loans:* Air mail; in some cases registered air mail.

    c) *Return of loans:* Air mail.

3. a) Requests for photoduplicated material should be sent to:

    Address as in 2a above.

    b) *Despatch of photoduplicated material:* Air mail.

4. *Restrictions:* Rare local material is not lent. Photocopies may be supplied if feasible.

5. *Request forms accepted:* Standard international request forms (eg IFLA) or official letters on headed paper.

6. Charges

    a) *Loans:* Postage may be charged in some cases, depending on weight.

    b) *Photoduplicated material:* $1.00 (Eastern Caribbean dollars) per copy; postage is additional.

    c) *35mm microfilm negative:*

    d) *35mm positive:*

    e) *Paper copy from microfilm:*   } No information given.

    f) *Duplicate microfiche:*

    g) *Paper copy from microfiche:*

7. Method of payment

    a) *Loans:* Postal order or bank draft payable to Accountant-General, Treasury Dept, Kingstown, St Vincent and the Grenadines.

    b) *Photoduplicated material:* Cheque, postal order or bank draft payable to Accountant-General, Treasury Dept, Kingstown, St Vincent and the Grenadines.

8. *Loan period:* 3 months.

9. *Renewal:* Allowed for up to 2 weeks on request.

SENEGAL

1. There has only been a national library since 1976. This is situated in Dakar in the Administrative Building of the National Archives.

2. a) Requests for loans should be sent to:

   Archives Nationales du Senegal
   Building Administratif
   Dakar

   Ecole Normale Supérieure de Dakar
   Bibliothèque
   Av. Bourguiba
   BP 5085

   Institut Fondamental d'Afrique Noire—CAD
   Bibliothèque
   BP 206
   Dakar

   b) *Despatch of loans:* Air mail.

   c) *Return of loans:* Air mail.

3. a) Requests for photoduplicated material should be sent to:

   IFAN-CAD
   BP 206
   Dakare

   ENSUT
   Bibliothèque
   Rue du Canif Claudel
   BP 5085
   Dakar

   ENS
   Bibliothèque
   Avenue Bourguiba
   BP 5056
   Dakar

   b) *Despatch of photoduplicated material:* Air mail.

4. *Restrictions:* Single-copy theses, manuscripts, rare and valuable books are not lent.

5. *Request forms accepted:* IFLA forms.

6. Charges

   a) *Loans:* Charges apply.

   b) *Photoduplicated material:* No information given.

   c) *35mm microfilm negative:* ⎫
   d) *35mm positive:* ⎬ Not applicable.

   e) *Paper copy from microfilm:* No information given.

   f) *Duplicate microfiche:* ⎫
   g) *Paper copy from microfiche:* ⎬ Not applicable.

7. Method of payment
   a) *Loans:*
   b) *Photoduplicated material:* } International Reply Coupons.

8. *Loan period:* One month.

9. *Renewal:* Allowed if requested before the end of the first month.

SEYCHELLES

1. There is no national system. Despite its name the National Library functions as a public library only:

   National Library
   P.O.Box 45
   Mahe

SIERRA LEONE

1. There is no national system.

2. a) There is no loan service.

3. a) Requests for photoduplicated material should be sent to:

   The Library
   Fourah Bay College
   Freetown

   b) *Despatch of photoduplicated material:* Air mail.

4. *Restrictions:* None.

5. *Request forms accepted:* Any.

6. Charges
   a) *Loans:* Not applicable.
   b) *Photoduplicated material:* Le 7.00c per page.
   c) *35mm microfilm negative:*
   d) *35mm positive:*
   e) *Paper copy from microfilm:* } Not applicable.
   f) *Duplicate microfiche:*
   g) *Paper copy from microfiche:*

7. Method of payment

   a) *Loans:* Not applicable.

   b) *Photoduplicated material:* Cheques to the Fourah Bay College Library account, Barclays Bank, Siaka Stevens St, Freetown or sent directly to the Library.

8. *Loan period:* ⎫
                ⎬ Not applicable.
9. *Renewal:* ⎭

SINGAPORE

1. The system is based on the reference and lending collection of the National Library. This collection covers all significant serials and reports and all English, Malay, Chinese and Tamil monographs.

2. a) Requests for loans should be sent to:

   Assistant Director
   Reference Services Division
   National Library Singapore
   Stamford Road
   Singapore 0617

                                    Telephone: 3377355
                                    Telex: RS 26620 NATLIB
                                    Fax: 3309611
                                    Telebox: GVT238 (3309609)

   b) *Despatch of loans:* Air mail.

   c) *Return of loans:* Air mail.

3. a) Requests for photoduplicated material should be sent to:

   Address as in 2a above.

   b) *Despatch of photoduplicated material:* Air mail.

4. *Restrictions:* Microfilm negatives, newspapers, maps, reference periodicals, (where photocopies may be supplied in lieu of loan) manuscripts, rare books, documents, audio-visual materials, restricted publications, materials in fragile condition, frequently used materials, microcomputer software, vertical resource files, Southeast Asia Collection items for which no duplicate copies are available and quick Reference Collection.

5. *Request forms accepted:* IFLA or ALA forms preferred.

6. Charges

   a) *Loans:* Postal costs.

   b) *Photoduplicated material:* S$ 0.30 per copy plus postage.

   c) *35mm microfilm negative:* S$ 0.30 per frame (from source materials)
                                           S$ 6.00 per metre or part thereof (not exceeding 15 metres) (duplicate)
                                             S$ 100.00 per reel of not more than 30 metres (exceeding 15 metres) (duplicate)

   d) *35mm positive:* S$ 0.30 per frame (from source materials)
                                           S$ 3.00 per metre or part thereof (not exceeding 15 metres).
                                           S$ 50.00 per reel of not more than 30 metres (exceeding 15 metres)

e) *Paper copy from microfilm:*

Photoprints	Electrostatic	Photographic
A4 (21cm x 29.7cm)	S$ 3.20 each	S$ 4.00 each
A3 (29.7cm x 42cm)	S$ 3.50 each	S$ 5.50 each
A2 (42cm x 59.4cm)	S$ 4.10 each	S$ 9.50 each
A1 (59.4cm x 84.1cm)		S$ 14.70 each

f) *Duplicate microfiche:*

g) *Paper copy from microfiche:* } Not applicable.

7. Method of payment

a) *Loans:*

b) *Photoduplicated material:* } Advance payment required in Singapore dollars by cheque or bank draft to the Director, National Library

8. *Loan period:* One month from date of receipt.

9. *Renewal:* Not normally allowed.

SOLOMON ISLANDS

1. National lending is done on an internal form and is usually requests from provincial libraries. The National Library is responsible for sending out book boxes to schools, missions and households in remote areas.

    International requests are made to the National Library of Australia, using their interloan request forms. Requests to other libraries are made only rarely, and are by letter.

    There is no usable union catalogue, or national guidelines. The Pacific Collection handles all interloans to the National Library either coming or going. This state of affairs has come about because the PC holds the items most likly to be requested. Other libraries deal with interloans independently from the National Library. There are a number of special libraries, with on-line facilities, fax, etc which handle specialised requests eg Dodo Creek Agricultural Research Station, ICLARM Research Station (marine biology, notably giant clams), Forestry Research Centre, Munda, South Pacific Forum Fisheries Agency. Some of the other Ministries have small collections, and can, in theory, do their own interloans, eg Ministry of Agriculture and Labour, Trade and Commerce, Natural Resources.

2. a) Requests for loans should be sent to:

    National Library
    P.O.Box 165
    Honiara   **Telephone: 21601**

    b) *Despatch of loans:* Air mail.

    c) *Return of loans:* Air mail.

3. a) Requests for photoduplicated material should be sent to:

    Address as in 2a above.

    b) *Despatch of photoduplicated material:* Air mail.

4. *Restrictions:* Older materials not lent but copies may be possible.

5. *Request forms accepted:* Any.

6. Charges

   a) *Loans:* Postal costs.

   b) *Photoduplicated material:* 20c (Solomon Islands currency).

   c) *35mm microfilm negative:*

   d) *35mm positive:*

   e) *Paper copy from microfilm:* $\Big\}$ Not applicable.

   f) *Duplicate microfiche:*

   g) *Paper copy from microfiche:*

7. Method of payment

   a) *Loans:* No information given.

   b) *Photoduplicated material:* Payment with order.

8. *Loan period:* 3 weeks depending on where the material is going.

9. *Renewal:* Not allowed.

SOUTH AFRICA

1. The State Library acts as the national and international centre for interlending for Southern African libraries. The major catalogues are:

   —**SA Joint Catalogue of Monographs** comprising the holdings of approximately 400 libraries in Southern Africa (available on COM-fiche according to author, title and ISBN).

   —Periodical holdings are covered by the microfiche publication: **Periodicals in Southern African Libraries (PISAL)**

   Information from 1984 to date on the above catalogues is also available on the co-operative computerised database of SABINET (South African Bibliographic and Information Network).

   Policies and procedures are set out in the **Interlending Manual for Southern African Libraries** which is published by the State Library and updated regularly in loose-leaf format.

2. a) Requests for loans should be sent to:

   National Interlending Section
   The State Library
   P.O.Box 397
   Pretoria 0001

   Telephone: + 27 12 21–8931
   Telex: 3–22171 SA
   Answer back code: 4401
   Fax: + 27 12 325–5984

   b) *Despatch of loans:* Registered air mail.

   c) *Return of loans:* Air mail.

3. a) Requests for photoduplicated material should be sent to:

   Address as in 2a above.

   b) *Despatch of photoduplicated material:* Air mail.

4. *Restrictions:* None.

5. *Request forms accepted:* IFLA forms preferred. A photocopy of the source of reference should be supplied if possible.

6. Charges

   a) *Loans:* Air mail costs are reclaimed. A handling fee of R25,00 per request is charged for all interlending requests received from overseas libraries.

   b) *Photoduplicated material:* Copies of 10 pages or less are supplied free of charge.

   11–25 pages: R15,00
   26–40 pages: R20,00
   41–55 pages: R25,00, etc
   For 11 pages or more a R25,00 handling fee per request is charged.
   A price limit in US Dollars or Pound Sterling should be supplied.

   c) *35mm microfilm negative:*

   d) *35mm positive:*

   } Actual cost plus postage and handling fee.

   e) *Paper copy from microfilm:* Same charges as in 6b above.

   f) *Duplicate microfiche:* R10,00 per fiche plus postage and handling.

   g) *Paper copy from microfiche:* Same charges as in 6b above.

7. Method of payment

   a) *Loans:*

   b) *Photoduplicated material:*

   } Invoices are sent after the despatch of the loan or photoduplicated documents. Payment can be made in International Reply Coupons or South African Rand. Estimates are supplied on request.

8. *Loan period:* One month from date of receipt.

9. *Renewal:* Not normally possible.

10. *Additional information:* All requests for loans or photoduplicated documents should be sent to the State Library, Pretoria.

BOPHUTHATSWANA

1–9 No information given. The address of the national library is:

Bophuthatswana National Library
Private Bag X 2004
Mafikent 8670
South Africa

CISKEI

1. The national and international system used is based on the guidelines set out by Pretoria State Library.

2. a) Requests for loans should be sent to:

   Ciskei National Library
   P/B X542 Zwelitsha 5608
   Republic of Ciskei   **Fax: 0401–91189**

   b) *Despatch of loans:* Air mail.

   c) *Return of loans:* Air mail.

3. a) Requests for photoduplicated material should be sent to:

   Address as in 2a above.

   b) *Despatch of photoduplicated material:* Air mail.

4. *Restrictions:* Reference material and Africana.

5. *Request forms accepted:* IFLA forms preferred.

6. Charges

   a) *Loans:* Free.

   b) *Photoduplicated material:* 20c.

   c) *35mm microfilm negative:* ⎫
   d) *35mm positive:* ⎭ Not applicable.

   e) *Paper copy from microfilm:* 20c.

   f) *Duplicate microfiche:* ⎫
   g) *Paper copy from microfiche:* ⎭ Not applicable.

7. Method of payment

   a) *Loans:* ⎫
   b) *Photoduplicated material:* ⎭ Coupons.

8. *Loan period:* One month.

9. *Renewal:* Allowed.

TRANSKEI

1. There is no national system yet. It is part of the South African State library system. The address of the national library is:

   Transkei National Library Service
   Private Bag X5095
   Umtata
   Transkei
   South Africa

VENDA

1. All libraries wishing to become members of the South African loans network can register and pay the required fee. The scheme is open also for libraries of neighbouring territories. Mainly two bibliographies are used for this purpose, the **Joint Catalogue of Monographs Microfiche** and the **South African Union Catalogue**. Copies of national guidelines are obtained from the Interlibrary Loans Division of the State Library in Pretoria.

    The interlending scheme is such that the requesting library can write directly to the holding library and need not use the Centre.

    Though Venda National Library is a library of a South African Independent National State it was only established in 1979 and is still very much dependent on the South African State Library. No interlibrary loan system operates in Venda because only two real libraries exist—the National Library and the University Library. Venda National Library is also not involved in international lending.

SPAIN

1. The system is based on the stock of the Biblioteca Nacional.

2. a) Requests for loans should be sent to:

    Servicio de Prestamo Interbibliotecario
    Biblioteca Nacional
    Paseo de Recoletos 20
    28001 Madrid   **Telephone: 34–1–27568 00**

    b) *Despatch of loans:* Air mail overseas.

    c) *Return of loans:* Air mail required from overseas.

3. a) Requests for photoduplicated material should be sent to:

    Servicio de Reprografia
    Biblioteca Nacional
    Paseo de Recoletos 20
    28001 Madrid

    b) *Despatch of photoduplicated material:* Air mail overseas.

4. *Restrictions:* Only duplicates after 1940 are lent. Manuscripts, rare books, periodicals and monographs before 1940 can be supplied by photocopy, microfiche or microfilm.

5. *Request forms accepted:* IFLA forms preferred.

6. Charges

    a) *Loans:* Postal costs.

    b) *Photoduplicated material:* 8 pesetas per page; minimum of 80 pesetas.

    c) *35mm microfilm negative:* 10 pesetas per exposure; minimum of 100 pesetas.

    d) *35mm positive:* No information given.

    e) *Paper copy from microfilm:* 12 pesetas per page; minimum charge of 120 pesetas.

    f) *Duplicate microfiche:* ⎫
                                      ⎬ No information given.
    g) *Paper copy from microfiche:* ⎭

7. Method of payment

   a) *Loans:* Postage to be refunded by International Reply Coupons.

   b) *Photoduplicated material:* Invoices are supplied. Payment can be made by a cheque payable in a Spanish bank or by bank transfer to the 'Banco Espanol de Credito', Plaza de la Independencia No 4, Madrid. Account Number 10.285/271; directed to 'Servicio de Reprografia de la Biblioteca Nacional.'

8. *Loan period:* One month.

9. *Renewal:* Allowed but application should be made before the end of the existing loan period.

10. *Additional information:* Items will be sent direct to the requesting library; returned loans should be sent direct to the lending library.

    The interlibrary loan service is being reorganised.

SRI LANKA

1. National and international lending systems are based on the collections and Union Catalogue of current acquisitions of major libraries in the country, mainly in the social sciences and humanities. National guidelines will be formulated by the National Library in due course. If it cannot satisfy a request, it will act as a referral centre.

2. a) Requests for loans should be sent to:

   Director
   Sri Lanka National Library Services Board
   P.O.Box 1764
   6, Independence Avenue
   Colombo 07   **Telephone: 698847, 68198, 68199, 685203, 68201, 685200, 685195**

   Assistant Librarian
   Reader Services
   P.O.Box 35
   The Library
   University of Peradeniya   **Telephone: 08 88301 Ext 240**

   b) *Despatch of loans:* Second class air mail.

   c) *Return of loans:* Air mail.

3. a) Requests for photoduplicated material should be sent to:

   Addresses as in 2a above.

   b) *Despatch of photoduplicated material:* Air mail.

4. *Restrictions:* The legal deposit collection, rare books and manuscripts will not be sent on loan but photoduplicated copies can be sent. The University Library does not lend periodicals and unpublished theses are lent only upon the signature on a declaration form by the requesting library and reader.

5. *Request forms accepted:* IFLA forms preferred.

6. Charges

   a) *Loans:* Postage costs are charged if they exceed RS 35.00 (equivalent to one US dollar).

   b) *Photoduplicated material:* A4 one side: RS 1.50
      A4 both sides: RS 3.00
      B4 one side: RS 2.00
      B4 both sides: RS 3.50

   c) *35mm microfilm negative:* RS 615 for 100 ft reel.

   d) *35mm positive:* RS 440 for 100 ft reel.

   e) *Paper copy from microfilm:* One side: RS 3.75.
      Both sides: RS 7.15

   f) *Duplicate microfiche:* RS 35 per fiche.

   g) *Paper copy from microfiche:* RS 5 per page. Microform not available from the University of Peradeniya.

7. Method of payment

   a) *Loans:* No information given.

   b) *Photoduplicated material:* Copying fee should be paid in advance (University of Peradeniya).

8. *Loan period:* One month.

9. *Renewal:* One extension of one month is granted on request (if it is not in high demand or if multiple copies are available in the collection).

SUDAN*

1. Interlibrary lending within the Sudan is conducted by special arrangement between the libraries concerned. Interlending with foreign libraries is not available at present. However, it may be possible for foreign libraries to obtain material through:

   The National Documentation Centre
   National Council for Research
   Khartoum

   This Centre has published a union list of periodicals in the Sudan.

SURINAME

1. There is no national system and no national centre. However, the Anton de Kom University of Suriname Library is willing to serve as such and will try to satisfy requests.

2. a) Requests for loans should be sent to:

   Anton de Kom University of Suriname Library
   P.O.Box 9212   Telephone: 597–65558
                                              597–64547
                                 Telex: ADEKUS 311 SN

b) *Despatch of loans:* Air mail.

c) *Return of loans:* Air mail.

3. a) Requests for photoduplicated material should be sent to:

   Address as in 2a above.

   b) *Despatch of photoduplicated material:* Air mail.

4. *Restrictions:* Rare books are not loaned.

5. *Request forms accepted:* IFLA forms or similar.

6. Charges

   a) *Loans:* Postal costs are not currently charged. However, if the number of requests increases, charging may be necessary.

   b) *Photoduplicated material:* $0.50 per page.

   c) *35mm microfilm negative:*

   d) *35mm positive:*

   e) *Paper copy from microfilm:* } Not applicable.

   f) *Duplicate microfiche:*

   g) *Paper copy from microfiche:*

7. Method of payment

   a) *Loans:* Not applicable.

   b) *Photoduplicated material:* Cheque or bank draft.

8. *Loan period:* One month.

9. *Renewal:* Allowed unless the item is needed by another user.

SWAZILAND

1. The system is based on the National Library and the University Library both of which are part of the Southern African System in turn based on the State Library of Pretoria.

2. a) Requests for loans should be sent to:

   Interlending Section
   Swaziland National Library
   P.O.Box 1461
   Mbabane

   b) *Despatch of loans:* Air mail.

   c) *Return of loans:* Air mail.

3. a) Requests for photoduplicated material should be sent to:

   Address as in 2a above.

   b) *Despatch of photoduplicated material:* Air mail.

4. *Restrictions:* Library material in heavy use and reference books are not lent.

5. *Request forms accepted:* Standard interlending forms (postal, telex and fax).

6. Charges

   a) *Loans:* Free.

   b) *Photoduplicated material:* 20 cents per page or copy.

   c) *35mm microfilm negative:* E 1.00 per exposure.

   d) *35mm positive:* No information given.

   e) *Paper copy from microfilm:* E 1.00

   f) *Duplicate microfiche:* E 2.00 per fiche.

   g) *Paper copy from microfiche:* No information given.

7. Method of payment

   a) *Loans:* Not applicable.

   b) *Photoduplicated material:* Exchange coupons.

8. *Loan period:* One month from date of receipt.

9. *Renewal:* Allowed unless there has been another request for the item.

10. *Additional information:* Items are sent direct to the requesting library and should be returned direct to the lending library.

SWEDEN

1. The Swedish interlending system is decentralised. The most complete collection of Swedish imprints belongs to Kung Biblioteket (The Royal Library) and is not available for international lending. Questions concerning Swedish imprints may preferably be sent to Kungl Biblioteket and requests for photocopies are similarly accepted. However, in 1979 Lund Universitetsbibliotek (University Library of Lund) was given the status of second national library. The responsibility for the loan of Swedish imprints to foreign countries was transferred to Lunds Universitetsbibliotek. The major research libraries (which have legal deposit collections) and a few special libraries also offer international lending services.

2. a) Requests for loans should be sent to:

   Uppsala Universitetsbibliotek
   Box 510
   S-751 20 Uppsala   **Telex: 76076 UBUPPS S**

   Göteborgs Universitetsbibliotek
   Box 5096
   S-402 22 Göteborg   **Telex: 20896 UBGBG S**

   Stockholms Universitetsbiblioteket med
   Kungl Vetenskapsakademiens Bibliotek
   S-106 91 Stockholm   **Telex: 11734 UNIVER S**

   Umeå Universitetsbibliotek
   Box 718
   S-901 10 Umeå   **Telex: 54060 UBUMEA S**

   Linköpings Universitetsbibliotek
   S-581 83 Linköping   **Telex: 50067 LINBIBL S**

Requests for medical literature should be sent to:

Karolinska Institutets Bibliotek
Box 60201
S-104 01 Stockholm   **Telex: 17179 KIBIC S**

Requests for technical literature should be sent to:

Tekniska Högskolans Bibliotek
Fack
S-100 44 Stockholm   **Telex: 10389 KTHB S**

   (i)   **Humanities, social sciences and theology**

       University Library, Dept 1
       Box 3
       S-221 00 Lund   **Telephone: 046–109188**
                                         Telex: 32208

   (ii) Natural sciences, medicine and technology

       University Library, Dept 2
       Box 3
       221 00 Lund   **Telephone: 046–109237**
                                       Telex: 33248 Fax: 110019

  b) *Despatch of loans:* Europe: Surface mail.
                               Outside Europe: Air mail.

  c) *Return of loans:* Items sent by air mail should be returned by air mail.

3.   a) Requests for photoduplicated material should be sent to:

      Addresses as in 2a above plus:

      Kungl Biblioteket (The Royal Library)
      Låneexpeditionen
      Box 5039
      S-102 41 Stockholm

   b) *Despatch of photoduplicated material:* Air mail (University Library of Lund).

4.   *Restrictions:* There are certain restrictions for loan: rare books, material older than 1700, books whose size or weight make them not fit for postal handling etc, are not available for international loan. Certain categories, for instance fiction books printed in Sweden, are available only for reading room use in the borrowing library.

     Xerox-copying of old, rare or for other reasons particularly valuable material is not allowed.

     (These restrictions apply to the University of Lund).

5.   *Request forms accepted:* IFLA forms from countries outside Scandinavia and Scandinavian interlibrary forms from Scandinavian countries (University Library of Lund).

6.   Charges

     The costs below apply to the University Library of Lund.

   a) *Loans:* Free.

   b) *Photoduplicated material:* 30 Swedish Crowns for sets containing 1 to 10 xerox copies. Customers with deposit accounts pay 20 Swedish Crowns for these sets.

   c) *35mm microfilm negative:* 4 Swedish Crowns per frame.

   d) *35mm positive:* 6 Swedish Crowns per page.

   e) *Paper copy from microfilm:* 15 Swedish Crowns (21 x 29.7cm).

   f) *Duplicate microfiche:*   }
                                Not applicable.
   g) *Paper copy from microfiche:* }

7. Method of payment

   a) *Loans:* Not applicable.

   b) *Photoduplicated material:* Invoice sent with the material.

8. *Loan period:* Usually 30 days.

9. *Renewal:* Generally allowed unless the item is required by another user.

10. *Additional information:* Since 1990 Swedish university libraries have to pay postal fees for all despatches. A governmental investigation is going on as to whether libraries will have to charge borrowing libraries for the postal costs involved.

SWITZERLAND

1. The system is based on the Swiss Union Catalogue (foreign publications held by Swiss libraries) and the Swiss National Library ('Helvetica').

   The Swiss Union Catalogue (Catalogue collectif suisse) serves the function of an International Loan Centre and has direct connections with libraries and regional union catalogues in other cities (Zurich, Basel, Lausanne, etc).

   Leitfaden des interbibliothekarischen Leihverkehrs = Guide du prêt interbibliothèques Aufl/4ème éd, Berne, Catalogue collectif suisse, 1986 253pp can be obtained from the Swiss National Library.

2. a) Requests for loans should be sent to:

   Catalogue collectif suisse
   Bibliothèque nationale suisse
   Hallwylstrasse 15
   CH—3003 Berne

   Telephone: (+ +41 33) 61 89 42
   Telex: 32526 SLBBE CH
   Fax: (+ +41 31) 61 84 63

   b) *Despatch of loans:* Air mail outside Europe.

   c) *Return of loans:* Air mail required from outside Europe.

3. a) Requests for photoduplicated material should be sent to:

   Address as in 2a above.

   b) *Despatch of photoduplicated material:* Air mail outside Europe.

4. *Restrictions:* Very old or valuable monographs are not lent. Serials are not lent as a rule (if bound in heavy volumes or recent editions in high demand). Photocopies can be supplied.

5. *Request forms accepted:* IFLA forms preferred.

6. Charges

   a) *Loans:* Free of charge for Helvetica.

   b) *Photoduplicated material:* 1–10 pages: SFr 10.00 + postage

   c) *35mm microfilm negative:*

   d) *35mm positive:*
   } 1–10 frames: SFr 10.00 + postage
   Each additional frame: SFr 0.30

   e) *Paper copy from microfilm:* 1–10 pages: SFr 15.00 + postage
   Each additional copy: SFr 1.00

   f) *Duplicate microfiche:*

   g) *Paper copy from microfiche:*
   } Not applicable

7. Method of payment

   a) *Loans:* Postage refunds may be waived by mutual agreement.

   b) *Photoduplicated material:* Invoice sent with item. Payment by International Reply Coupons or international money order according to country.

8. *Loan period:* 4 weeks from date of receipt.

9. *Renewal:* Allowed.

10. *Additional information:* Items should be sent direct to the requesting library.

SYRIA

1. There is no international or national lending system but Assad National Library will supply photocopies or microforms of items in its collection.

2. There is no loan service.

3. a) Requests for photoduplicated material should be sent to:

   Assad National Library
   P.O.Box 3639
   Damascus   **Telephone: 338255**
                                                    Telex: 419134

   b) *Despatch of photoduplicated material:* No information given.

4. *Restrictions:*

5. *Request forms accepted:*   No information given.

6. Charges

   a) *Loans:* Not applicable.

   b) *Photoduplicated material:*

   c) *35mm microfilm negative:*

   d) *35mm positive:*

   e) *Paper copy from microfilm:*   No information given.

   f) *Duplicate microfiche:*

   g) *Paper copy from microfiche:*

7. Method of payment

   a) *Loans:* Not applicable.

   b) *Photoduplicated material:* Exchange of a new edition of a scientific book or pre-payment.

8. *Loan period:*

                          Not applicable.
9. *Renewal:*

116

TANZANIA*

1. The system is based on the University Library stock plus a union catalogue for periodicals.

2. a) Requests for loans should be sent to:

    University Library
    P.O.Box 35092
    Dar es Salaam

    b) *Despatch of loans:* Air mail.

    c) *Return of loans:* Air mail.

3. a) Requests for photoduplicated material should be sent to:

    Address as in 2a above.

    b) *Despatch of photoduplicated material:* Air mail.

4. *Restrictions:* Periodicals, theses and items in the 'East Africana' Collection (of which there is only one copy) are not lent. Photocopies of parts of these works can be supplied.

5. *Request forms accepted:* Any.

6. Charges

    a) *Loans:*

    b) *Photoduplicated material:*

    c) *35mm microfilm negative:*

    d) *35mm positive:* No information given.

    e) *Paper copy from microfilm:*

    f) *Duplicate microfiche:*

    g) *Paper copy from microfiche:*

7. Method of payment

    a) *Loans:* Invoices for photocopying and/or postage are usually sent a few days after the item requested.

    b) *Photoduplicated material:*

8. *Loan period:* One month from date of receipt.

9. *Renewal:* No information given.

10. *Additional information:* Items will be sent as directed and should be returned direct to the lending library.

THAILAND

1. The National Library is the centre of the network of exchange and interlibrary loans of library material in Thailand. It is a member of NLDC-SEA Consortium. There is no lending collection but photocopy, microfilm and microjacket services are available. The National Library is also the Secretarial Office of THAI NATIS and Humanities Information Network Center.

2.   There is no loan service.

3.   a)   Requests for photoduplicated material should be sent to:

National Library of Thailand
Samsen Road
Bangkok 10300   **Telex: 84189 DEPFIAR TH**

b)   *Despatch of photoduplicated material:* Air mail.

4.   *Restrictions:* Material of danger to national security.

5.   *Request forms accepted:* IFLA forms.

6.   Charges

a)   *Loans:* Not applicable.

b)   *Photoduplicated material:* US$ 5.00 or Bahts 125.00 for one journal article, including postage. Bahts 2.00 for each additional page (plus postage).

c)   *35mm microfilm negative:* Bahts 4000.00, not including postage.

d)   *35mm positive:* Bahts 3,000.00, not including postage.

e)   *Paper copy from microfilm:* Bahts 20.00, not including postage.

f)   *Duplicate microfiche:* Bahts 60.00, not including postage.

g)   *Paper copy from microfiche:* Not applicable.

7.   Method of payment

a)   *Loans:* Not applicable.

b)   *Photoduplicated material:* Proforma invoice.

8.   *Loan period:* ⎱
                      ⎰ Not applicable.
9.   *Renewal:* ⎰

10. *Additional information:* The National Library of Thailand is also the UNESCO/PGI Publications Clearing House and Document Supply Service for ASIA/Pacific and national coordinator for ASTINFO Document Delivery Pilot Project, for which the national Library of Australia is the Regional Coordinator.

TOGO

1.   There is no national or international interlending or copying system. Loans are made between libraries but there is no proper system. The National Library is in the process of starting a national system of interlibrary loan by the creation of an Association of Libraries. Its address is:

Bibliothèque Nationale
Avenue de la Victoire
BP 1002
Lome

TONGA

1. There is no national system and no national library.

TRINIDAD AND TOBAGO

1. There is no national system and no national library.

TUNISIA

1. The system is based on the Tunisian National Library.

2. a) Requests for loans should be sent to:

    **Bibliothèque Nationale
    20 Souk El Attarine
    Tunis, BP 42**

    b) *Despatch of loans:* Air mail.

    c) *Return of loans:* Air mail.

3. a) Requests for photoduplicated material should be sent to:

    **Bibliothèque Nationale
    Service des Exchanges et Dons
    44, Rue Charles de Gaulle
    Tunis**

    b) *Despatch of photoduplicated material:* Air mail.

4. *Restrictions:* Items in poor condition will not be photocopied.

5. *Request forms accepted:* IFLA forms.

6. Charges

    a) *Loans:* Free.

    b) *Photoduplicated material:* 30 millimes per page.

    c) *35mm microfilm negative:* ⎫
    d) *35mm positive:* ⎭ 300 millimes per page.

    e) *Paper copy from microfilm:* No information given.

    f) *Duplicate microfiche:* ⎫
    g) *Paper copy from microfiche:* ⎭ Not available.

7. Method of payment

    a) *Loans:* Not applicable.

    b) *Photoduplicated material:* International Reply Coupons.

8. *Loan period:* One month.

9. *Renewal:* Renewal of 15 days is possible.

TURKEY

1. The system is based on union catalogues and the collections of the National Library.

2. a) Requests for loans should be sent to:

   Millî Kütüphane (National Library)
   Bahçelievler
   Ankara   **Telephone: 2224148, 2223812**
                                        Fax: 2230451

   b) *Despatch of loans:* Air mail.

   c) *Return of loans:* Air mail.

3. a) Requests for photoduplicated material should be sent to:

   Millî Kütüphane (National Library)
   Uluslararasi Ilişkiler (International Relations)
   Bahçelievler
   Ankara   **Telephone: 2224768**

   b) *Despatch of photoduplicated material:* Air mail.

4. *Restrictions:* No significant restrictions.

5. *Request forms accepted:* Any.

6. Charges

   a) *Loans:* A charge may be made depending on weight and distance. Postage is usually reclaimed.

   b) *Photoduplicated material:* 200.TL. per page.

   c) *35mm microfilm negative:* ⎫
                                  ⎬ 760.TL.
   d) *35mm positive:*)   ⎭

   e) *Paper copy from microfilm:* 200.TL.

   f) *Duplicate microfiche:* 250.TL.

   g) *Paper copy from microfiche:* 200.TL.

7. Method of payment

   a) *Loans:* Postage may be paid by International Reply Coupons.

   b) *Photoduplicated material:* $US or DM.

8. *Loan period:* One month.

9. *Renewal:* Renewal of 15 days may be granted.

TUVALU

1. There is no national system and no union catalogue. The address of the National Library is:

    National Library and Archives of Tuvalu
    P.O.Box 36
    Funafuti Island
    Tuvalu   **Telephone: 711**
                                                   Telex: TV COMM 4800

UGANDA

1. There is no national system yet. However, Makerere University Library Service for a long time has been using the British Library Document Supply Centre to obtain photocopies of articles. Similarly it sometimes supplies photocopies of required materials to the Centre and other people, mainly in Europe, North America and Africa, plus a few to other countries.

    Interlending among Ugandan libraries is difficult because of the poor postal system. Demands of readers are usually met by photocopying.

2. There is no loan service.

3. a) Requests for photoduplicated material should be sent to:

    Makerere University
    Main Library
    P.O.Box 7062
    Kampala

    b) *Despatch of photoduplicated material:* Air mail.

4. *Restrictions:* Theses and manuscripts.

5. *Request forms accepted:* IFLA forms.

6. Charges

    a) *Loans:* Not applicable.

    b) *Photoduplicated material:* Shs. 50/- per page (U$ 12 cents).

    c) *35mm microfilm negative:*

    d) *35mm positive:*

    e) *Paper copy from microfilm:*   Not applicable.

    f) *Duplicate microfiche:*

    g) *Paper copy from microfiche:*

7. Method of payment

    a) *Loans:* Not applicable.

    b) *Photoduplicated material:* Cash or cheque.

8. *Loan period:*
                        Not applicable.
9. *Renewal:*

UNION OF SOVIET SOCIALIST REPUBLICS

1. The USSR interlending system is based on coordination and cooperation between Soviet libraries. International lending in the USSR is conducted by 134 libraries which possess universal or special collections. The major libraries participating in international lending are All-Union Centres of Interlending, the State libraries of the Union's republics, the libraries of the Academies of Science of the republics and some university libraries. The Lenin State Library acts as the coordinating centre for international lending. Other libraries of the USSR obtain international loans for their readers through libraries which participate in international lending. The international lending system is supported by national and regional union catalogues.

2. a) Requests for loans should be sent to:

    The Lenin State Library of the USSR
    Prospekt Kalinina, 3
    101000 Moscow   **Telex: 411167 GBL SU**

    b) *Despatch of loans:* Air mail outside Europe.

    c) *Return of loans:* Air mail from outside Europe.

3. a) Requests for photoduplicated material should be sent to:

    Address as in 2a above.

    b) *Despatch of photoduplicated material:* Air mail outside Europe.

4. *Restrictions:* The following materials are not lent:- manuscripts (including theses), illustrative materials, newspapers, items which by reason of size or weight cannot be transported, rare and precious items.

5. *Request forms accepted:* IFLA forms.

6. Charges

    a) *Loans:*

    b) *Photoduplicated material:*

    c) *35mm microfilm negative:*

    d) *35mm positive:*   Charges are made according to agreements with the libraries
                                            of other countries and may be free where there are reciprocal
    e) *Paper copy from microfilm:*   arrangements.

    f) *Duplicate microfiche:*

    g) *Paper copy from microfiche:*

7. Method of payment

    a) *Loans:* Usually International Reply Coupons for postage refund.

    b) *Photoduplicated material:* Usually International Reply Coupons.

8. *Loan period:* Printed matter: one month.
                    Microfilms: 45 days from date of receipt.

9. *Renewal:* Allowed unless the item is in demand elsewhere.

10. *Additional information:* Documents are sent by the supplying library and should be returned to them.

UNITED ARAB EMIRATES

1. There is no national system. The address of the national library is:

    National Library
    Cultural Centre
    P.O.Box 7480
    Abu Dhabi

UNITED KINGDOM

1. The system is based on a central lending collection covering all significant serials and reports and all significant recent English language monographs, supported by national and regional union catalogues and several large libraries.

2. a) Requests for loans should be sent to:

    Requests
    British Library Document Supply Centre
    Boston Spa, Wetherby
    West Yorkshire LS23 7BQ

    Telephone: (0937) 843434
    Telex: 557381 BLDSC G
    Fax: (0937) 546333

    Automated Request Transmission (ART) facilities are available. Requests may be transmitted by telex, computer or via the following database hosts: BLAISE-LINE ORDER, DIALOG-DIALORDER, DIMDI ORDER, QUESTORDER and ORBDOC.

    b) *Despatch of loans:* Air mail.

    c) *Return of loans:* Air mail.

3. a) Requests for photoduplicated material should be sent to:

    Address as in 2a above.

    b) *Despatch of photoduplicated material:* Air mail.

4. *Restrictions:* Monographs other than British will be lent only if in central stock (ie no search will be made in other libraries) and if not in demand in the UK. In additional Doctoral theses covered by **Dissertation Abstracts International** cannot be lent abroad, neither can photocopies or microfilm of these be provided for retention.

5. *Request forms accepted:* British Library Document Supply Centre pre-paid loan forms and photocopy forms with pre-paid photocopy coupons are preferred.

6&7 Charges and method of payment: The British Library Document Supply Centre operates two distinct international services:

    International Loan Service

    The International Loan Service is restricted to selected libraries of national standing. Pre-paid request forms are used.

    International Photocopy Service

    The International Photocopy Service is available to organisations and individuals and uses a pre-paid coupon system. Each coupon is valid for a photocopy to up to 10 pages of the original item or 20 pages of microfilm.

Deposit accounts are available for those libraries wishing to send requests by Automated Request Transmission. Details of this and all other services, including current prices, may be obtained from Customer Services at the address above.

8.   *Loan period:* One month from date of receipt.

9.   *Renewal:* Renewal of four weeks will be granted unless item is required by another user.

UNITED STATES OF AMERICA

1.   There is no centralised lending or borrowing agency in the United States. US librarians requesting material act individually or as part of a network or consortium. Whenever possible US libraries request materials directly from local and regional libraries and use the Library of Congress as a last resort. When the Library of Congress is unable to fill a request it will attempt to recommend other locations. Foreign libraries use the Library of Congress primarily as a source of US publications, requesting non-US publications from the country of origin first. All libraries are expected to consult the National Union Catalog, Union List of Serials, and other manual and electronic bibliographies such as OCLC, AGRICOLA, to verify citations and determine locations before submitting a request direct to holding libraries. The Library of Congress and the National Agricultural Library follow the IFLA Guidelines and the latest edition of the US National Interlibrary Loan Code. NAL is also a participant in the Agricultural Libraries Network (AGLINET).

The following entries provide details of three major US libraries only.

A.   Library of Congress

2.   a)   Requests for loans should be sent to:

Loan Division
Library of Congress
Washington DC 20540   **Telephone: (202) 707–5444**
Fax: (202) 707–5986
OCLC: LCL (See NAD first)
RLIN: DCLW
Dialcom: ALANet LCLOAN

b)   *Despatch of loans:* Air mail.

c)   *Return of loans:* Air mail.

3.   a)   Requests for photoduplicated material should be sent to:

i)   Photocopies up to 25 exposures:

Address as in 2a above.

ii)   Requests over 25 exposures, multiple requests for the same material and extensive photo-copying and reproduction:

Photoduplication Service
Library of Congress
Washington DC 20540   **Telephone: (202) 707 5640**

The photoduplication service will send a cost estimate and require prepayment before filling the request.

b)   *Despatch of photoduplicated material:* Air mail (or any other arrangement made by the requesting library at the latter's expense).

4. *Restrictions:*

   i) Books

   The Library of Congress will lend most material in the general book collection. Materials not available for borrowing include publications pre-1801, genealogy and local history material, most music, and audio-visual material.

   ii) Periodicals:

   Interlibrary loan will provide complimentary photocopies of articles up to 25 exposures. The original issue is not available for borrowing. Requests for articles over 25 exposures should be sent directly to the Photoduplication Service at the above address.

   iii) Newspapers:

   The Library of Congress will lend up to 6 reels of microfilm per request.

   iv) Microforms:

   The Library of Congress will lend microforms filmed by LC; others are available selectively.

   v) Dissertations:

   LC will not lend dissertations when the film is available from other sources.

5. *Request forms accepted:*

   Each request should be submitted on a separate ALA or IFLA form, or electronically, providing the most exact identification available. The request should contain the source of citation and bibliographic verification. If no bibliographic verification is available, a copy of the patron's citation should be included.

6. Charges

   There is no charge or prior registration requirement for interlibrary loan services, including limited article copying, provided by the Loan Division. There is a charge for photocopying over 25 exposures, and requests for this material should be sent directly to the Photoduplication Service at the address listed in 3aii.

   a) *Loans:* Free.

   b) *Photoduplicated material:* Free up to 25 exposures. Over 25 exposures: $0.45 per exposure.

   c) *35mm microfilm negative:* $0.14 per exposure.

   d) *35mm positive:* $24.00 per reel.

   e) *Paper copy from microfilm:* $1.75 per foot. (Minimum charge: $15.00).

   f) *Duplicate microfiche:* $1.25. (Minimum charge per order: $7.00)

   g) *Paper copy from microfiche:* $0.50 per exposure.

7. Method of payment

   a) *Loans:* Not applicable.

   b) *Photoduplicated material:* Payment in advance or deposit account with the Photoduplication Service.

8. *Loan period:* One month.

9. *Renewal:* One renewal allowed.

B. National Agricultural Library

Requests should only be made to the National Agricultural Library (NAL) after other sources in the requesting country have been exhausted.

2. There is no loan service outside the USA.

3. a) Requests for photoduplicated material should be sent to:

USDA, National Agricultural Library
Lending Branch
Beltsville
Maryland 20705

ALANET: ALA1031 (System 41)
DIALCOM: NAL—Lending AGS3058 (System
57)
EASYLINK: 62031265
ONTYME: NAL/LB
OCLC: Symbol is AGL
TWX/Telex: 710–828–0506 NAL LEND
Answer back: USDA NAL
Fax: 301–344–3675

Requests must include authorisation for charging, copyright compliance or contain a statement that the document requested is for research only, the standard bibliographic source which lists the title as owned by NAL (if possible) and verification of periodical articles or the sources of the citation requested. For electronic mail requests, the complete name and address of the requestor must appear with each item requested. If the citation is from a NAL database (AGRICOLA, Bibliography of Agriculture, or the NAL Catalog) and the call number is given, this call number must be included on the requests.

   b) *Despatch of photoduplicated material:* Air mail.

4. *Restrictions:* The request must contain a statement of willingness to pay copying charges or state membership of AGLINET.

5. *Request forms accepted:* When a form is used other than electronic mail, IFLA and/or ALA forms are preferred. Requests are not generally accepted in letter format.

6. Charges

   a) *Loans:* Not applicable.

   b) *Photoduplicated material:* $5.00 for the first 10 pages;
Each additional 10 pages per title: $3.00.
Free photocopy of US imprints only is provided to AGLINET participants.

   c) *35mm microfilm negative:* $10.00 per NAL produced reel.

   d) *35mm positive:* $10.00 per NAL produced reel.

   e) *Paper copy from microfilm:* $5.00 for the first 10 pages. Each additional 10 pages: $3.00.

   f) *Duplicate microfiche:* $5.00 for the first fiche. Each additional fiche: $0.50.

   g) *Paper copy from microfiche:* $5.00 for the first 10 pages. Each additional 10 pages: $3.00.

7. Method of payment

   a) *Loans:* Not applicable.

   b) *Photoduplicated material:*

Payment should not be included with the request. NAL does not have the facilities to accept direct payment for filled requests. Coupons are not accepted. Invoices are issued quarterly by the National Technical Information Service (NTIS). Payment should accompany a copy of the invoice and be sent to NTIS. Clients may establish a deposit account by contacting: National Technical Information Service, 5285 Port Royal Road, Springfield, Virginia, USA 22161. Libraries may contact the Head, Lending Branch, regarding cooperative agreements for document delivery.

8. *Loan period:*
                        } Not applicable.
9. *Renewal:*

10. *Additional information:*

NAL should be viewed as a library of last resort and requestors are expected to try major university, national, provincial or regional libraries prior to sending requests to NAL. Requests for special services or exemptions from standard policy should be directed to the Head, Lending Branch.

C.   National Library of Medicine

2.   There is no loan service outside the USA.

3.   a)   Requests for photoduplicated material should be sent to:

Collection Access Section
National Library of Medicine
8600 Rockville Pike
Bethesda
Maryland 20894   **Telefax: 301–496–2809**
                                       Telex: 710–824–9616
                                       Answer back: DNLMBETHESDA

   b)   *Despatch of photoduplicated material:* Air mail.

4.   *Restrictions:* Some monographs printed before 1914 are supplied in the form of microfilm. Journal literature is supplied as photocopies. Requests for more than 50 pages are rejected.

5.   *Request forms accepted:* IFLA or ALA requests forms preferred: a minimum of 3 copies of the request should be provided.

6.   Charges

   a)   *Loans:* Not applicable.

   b)   *Photoduplicated material:* $9.00 per filled request for up to 50 pages.

   c)   *35mm microfilm negative:* ⎫

   d)   *35mm positive:* ⎬ Not yet determined.

   e)   *Paper copy from microfilm:* ⎭

   f)   *Duplicate microfiche:* ⎫ Not applicable.

   g)   *Paper copy from microfiche:)* ⎭

7.   Method of payment

   a)   *Loans:* Not applicable.

   b)   *Photoduplicated material:*

   Payment should not be included with the request. Invoices are issued quarterly. Payment should accompany copy of invoice and be sent to the collection agent named on the invoice. NLM does not have the facilities to accept direct payment for filled requests.

8.   *Loan period:* ⎫
                     ⎬ Not applicable.
9.   *Renewal:* ⎭

10.   *Additional information:*

Each item or part-item must be requested on a separate request form. Each request must include a statement of conformance to Copyright Law (or guidelines).

URUGUAY

1. There is no national system for interlending. Most libraries in the country make their own arrangements for interlending. The Centro Nacional de Documentación Científica, Técnica y Económica of the Biblioteca Nacional will supply photocopies and forward requests to other libraries where necessary. Loans from its stock are only made within the city of Montevideo.

2. There is no loan service.

3. a) Requests for photoduplicated material should be sent to:

    Centro Nacional de Documentación Científica, Técnica y Económica
    Biblioteca Nacional (CNDCTE)
    18 de Julio 1790
    Casilla de Correo 452
    Montevideo   **Telephone: 484172**

    b) *Despatch of photoduplicated material:* Air mail.

4. *Restrictions:* There are some restrictions on photocopying old items, single copies and works of art.

5. *Request forms accepted:* Any.

6. Charges

    a) *Loans:* Not applicable.

    b) *Photoduplicated material:*

    c) *35mm microfilm negative:*

    d) *35mm positive:*

    e) *Paper copy from microfilm:* — As state institutions CNDCTE and the National Library cannot make any charges for photoduplicated material.

    f) *Duplicate microfiche:*

    g) *Paper copy from microfiche:*

7. Method of payment

    a) *Loans:*

    b) *Photoduplicated material:* — Not applicable.

8. *Loan period:*

9. *Renewal:* — Not applicable.

VENEZUELA

1.   There is no national system.

2.   a)   Requests for loans should be sent to:

     Biblioteca Nacional
     Coordinación de Referencia e Información
     Apartado 6525
     Caracas 1010   **Telephone: 429218**
                                         427230
                                         Fax: 429218

     b)   *Despatch of loans:* Air mail.

     c)   *Return of loans:* Air mail.

3.   a)   Requests for photoduplicated material should be sent to:

     Address as in 2a above.

     b)   *Despatch of photoduplicated material:* Air mail.

4.   *Restrictions:* Unique copies of material, rare books, manuscripts and reference books are not lent.

5.   *Request forms accepted:* IFLA forms preferred.

6.   Charges

     a)   *Loans:* Postal costs plus service.

     b)   *Photoduplicated material:* US $0.20 per page.

     c)   *35mm microfilm negative:* US $75.

     d)   *35mm positive:* US $28.

     e)   *Paper copy from microfilm:* US $0.25.

     f)   *Duplicate microfiche:* US $0.25.

     g)   *Paper copy from microfiche:* US $0.25.

7.   Method of payment

     a)   *Loans:*
                              } Cheques in US dollars.
     b)   *Photoduplicated material:*

8.   *Loan period:* One month.

9.   *Renewal:* Allowed unless material is likely to be requested elsewhere.

VIRGIN ISLANDS (UK)

1.   The Library Services Department, British Virgin Islands, does not have a formal system for interlending. At the National level the structure comprises the Main Library and Headquarters of the Library Service, and four Branch Libraries. Cataloguing, acquisitions, disbursements and a few of the other procedures are centralised.

If one of the Branch Libraries needs a book or other material from the Headquarters it is despatched for an unlimited period and recalled if it is needed by a patron at Headquarters. It is a very informal arrangement at the national level.

At the regional and international level, books would be lent to overseas libraries on request (with certain qualifications).

There is also an informal lending arrangement (ie requests are often made by telephone) with the nearby United States Virgin Islands Libraries since this is where most of the interlending requests originate.

Most of the time copies of the publication/material is supplied free if extra copies are available. If the material is not in stock for some reason, but it is available locally, if desired, the Library Service Department would purchase it and charge the requesting library for the material at cost-price.

2.   a)   Requests for loans should be sent to:

       Chief Librarian
       Library Services Department
       Government of the BVIS
       Road Town
       Tortola   **Telephone: 1 809 4943428**
                                             Telex: 7959 CENAD
                                             Fax: 1 809 4944435

   b)   *Despatch of loans:* Air mail.

   c)   *Return of loans:* Air mail.

3.   a)   Requests for photoduplicated material should be sent to:

       Address as in 2a above.

   b)   *Despatch of photocopies:* Air mail.

4.   *Restrictions:* Material in reference or Local History Collections is not lent.

       No photocopying over 50 pages is done.

5.   *Request forms accepted:* Any.

6.   Charges

   a)   *Loans:* No postal charges but cost price of material, if it is purchased specially.

   b)   Photoduplicated material: 10 cents (letter size)
                                       20 cents (A3 size)

   c)   *35mm microfilm negative:*

   d)   *35mm positive:*

   e)   *Paper copy from microfilm:*   } Not applicable.

   f)   *Duplicate microfiche:*

   g)   *Paper copy from microfiche:*

7.   Method of payment

   a)   *Loans:*   } Money order only, payable to

   b)   Photoduplicated materials: 'Accountant General'

8.   *Loan period:* One month.

9.   *Renewal:* Allow   e.

VIRGIN ISLANDS (US)

1. There is no national system but three libraries are involved in interlibrary lending.

2. a) Requests for loans should be sent to:

   University of the Virgin Islands
   St Croix Campus Library
   RR02, Box 10,000
   Kingshill
   St Croix
   US Virgin Islands 00850   Telephone: (809) 778–1620
                                        Fax: (809) 778–9168

   Ralph M Paiewonsky Library
   University of the Virgin Islands
   St Thomas
   US Virgin Islands 00802   Telephone: (809) 776–9200
                                        Fax: (809) 776–2399

   Enid M Baa Public Library
   23 Dronningens Gade
   St Thomas
   US Virgin Islands 00801   Telephone: (809) 774–0630
                                        Fax: (809) 775–1887

   The following information applies to the University of the Virgin Islands libraries only.

   b) *Despatch of loans:* Air mail.

   c) *Return of loans:* Air mail.

3. a) Requests for photoduplicated material should be sent to:

   Address as in 2a above.

   b) *Despatch of photoduplicated material:* Air mail.

4. *Restrictions:* Out of print and local material will not be loaned. If possible, it will be copied.

5. *Request forms accepted:* IFLA forms preferred.

6. Charges

   a) *Loans:* Charges apply plus replacement costs for lost or damaged materials.

   b) *Photoduplicated material:* $0.25.

   c) *35mm microfilm negative:* ⎤
                                   ⎬ Not applicable.
   d) *35mm positive:*   ⎦

   e) *Paper copy from microfilm:* $0.25.

   f) *Duplicate microfiche:* Not applicable.

   g) *Paper copy from microfiche:* $0.5.

7. Method of payment

   a) *Loans:*   ⎤ Invoices are sent with the items. Borrowing libraries
                                   ⎬ are expected to pay invoices plus postage costs.
   b) *Photoduplicated material:* ⎦

8. *Loan period:* 2 weeks from receipt of the item.

9. *Renewal:* Allowed.

WESTERN SAMOA

1.   There is no national system and no national library.

YEMEN

1.   Officially there is no interlending system. However, the University of Sanaa Library may be used as a centre for document supply at a minimum level. It is prepared to provide photocopies of any documents of international interest which it possesses.

2.   a)   Requests for loans should be sent to:

University of Sanaa
Central Library
P.O.Box 1247
Sanaa   **Telephone: 250507**
                                               Telex: 2803 UNISAN YE

     b)   *Despatch of loans:* Air mail.

     c)   *Return of loans:* Air mail.

3.   a)   Requests for photoduplicated material should be sent to:

          Address as in 2a above.

     b)   *Despatch of photoduplicated material:* Air mail.

4.   *Restrictions:* No information given.

5.   *Request forms accepted:* IFLA forms preferred.

6.   Charges

     a)   *Loans:* Postal costs.

     b)   *Photoduplicated material:* Costs exceeding US$10 are charged.

     c)   *35mm microfilm negative:* ⎫
                                      ⎬ Not applicable.
     d)   *35mm positive:*   ⎭

     e)   *Paper copy from microfilm:* Costs exceeding US$10 are charged.

     f)   *Duplicate microfiche:*   ⎫
                                          ⎬ Not applicable.
     g)   *Paper copy from microfiche:* ⎭

7.   Method of payment

     a)   *Loans:* No information given.

     b)   *Photoduplicated material:* Cheque.

8.   *Loan period:* ⎫
                     ⎬ No information given.
9.   *Renewal:*   ⎭

YUGOSLAVIA

1. There is no unified interlending system. All the national libraries of the republics and autonomous provinces as well as university libraries and libraries of the academies of sciences participate in international lending. Each national library maintains a union catalogue of its own area. The list below gives the addresses of all these libraries and further details of the main national libraries are given.

2. a) Requests for loans should be sent to:

    i) Serbia:

    Narodna biblioteka Srbije
    Služba za medjubibliotečku Pozajmicu
    11000 Beograd
    Skerlićeva 1   **Telephone: 011–451–242 Ext 64**
                                         011–452–952
                                         Telex: 12208

    ii) Croatia:

    Nacionalna i sveučilišna biblioteka
    41000 Zagreb
    Maruličev trg 21.
    pp 550   **Telephone: 041–446–322**
                                         Telex: 22206–YU-BICH

    iii) Slovenia:

    Narodna in univerzitetna knjižnica
    61001 Ljubljana
    Turjaška 1. pp 259   **Telephone: 061–332–853**
                                         Telex: 32285
                                         Fax: 061–332847
                                         E-mail: PAD: 220161130000;
                                         User: MEDBIBL

    iv) Kosovo:

    Narodna i univerzitetska biblioteka Kosova
    38000 Priština
    Ramiz Sadiku b.b   **Telephone: 038–22–782**

    v) Bosnia and Hercegovina:

    Narodna i univerzitetska biblioteka BiH
    71000 Sarajevo
    Obala 42   **Telephone: 071–532–204**
                                         Telex: 41477

    vi) Macedonia:

    Narodna i univerzitetska biblioteka 'Kliment Ohridski'
    91000 Skopje
    Goce Delčev 6   **Telephone: 091–232–122**

    vii) Montenegro:

    Centralna narodna bibloteka SR Crne Gore
    'Djurdje Crnojević'
    Bulevar Lenjina 163
    81250 Cetinje
    Njegoševa 1   **Telephone: 086–21–133**

viii) Vojvodina:

Biblioteka matice srpske
21000 Novi Sad
Ulica Matice Srpske 1

Telephone: Main exchange: 021–615–599
Library Information Dept: 021–28–747
Referral Centre: 021–28–574
                                021–28–859
Telex: 64367 BMS YU
Fax: 021 28574
E-mail: 3229, BMSNS (161140022 No YUPAC)

In addition:

ix) **Univerzitetna knjižnica Maribor**
62000 Maribor
Gospejna lo

Telephone: 062–25–851
Telex: 33328 YU UKM

x) **Univerzitetska biblioteka 'Svetozar Marković'**
11000 Beograd
Bulevar revolucije 71

Telephone: 011–325–067

xi) **Biblioteka Srpske akademije nauka i umetnosti**
11000 Beograd
Knez Mihailova 35

Telephone: 011–623–899

xii) **Biblioteka Jugoslavenske akademije znanosti in umjetnosti**
41000 Zagreb
Zrinski trg 11

Telephone: 041–433–444

A. **Narodna Biblioteka Srbije, Beograd**

The international lending service department loans books and produces photocopies and microfilms.

b) *Despatch of loans:* Registered mail.

c) *Return of loans:* Registered mail.

3. b) *Despatch of photoduplicated material:* Registered mail

4. *Restrictions:* Periodicals, old and rare books, handbooks, manuals, music sheets and notes are not lent but photocopies or microfilms may be made.

5. *Request forms accepted:* IFLA forms.

6. Charges

    a) *Loans:* Postal costs.

    b) *Photoduplicated material:* Under 10 copies: free.
                                  Over 10 copies: 30 dinar per page.

    c) *35mm microfilm negative:* } 8 dinar.
    d) *35mm positive:*

    e) *Paper copy from microfilm:* 38 dinar.

    f) *Duplicate microfiche:* } Not applicable.
    g) *Paper copy from microfiche:*

7. Method of payment

    a) *Loans:* } Dinars, foreign currency or International
    b) *Photoduplicated material:* } Reply Coupons.

8. *Loan period:* One month from date of receipt.

9. *Renewal:* Allowed if previously notified.

10. *Additional information:* The International Lending Service Department is not centralised; each library works independently for its users.

B. Nacionalna i sveučilišna Biblioteca, Zagreb

2. b) *Despatch of loans:* Registered surface mail.

    c) *Return of loans:* Air mail not required.

3. b) *Despatch of photoduplicated material:* Air mail outside Europe. Airmail only used on request within Europe.

4. *Restrictions:* None.

5. *Request forms accepted:* IFLA forms preferred.

6. Charges

    a) *Loans:* Postage costs.

    b) *Photoduplicated material:*

    c) *35mm microfilm negative:*

    d) *35mm positive:*

    e) *Paper copy from microfilm:*   No information given.

    f) *Duplicate microfiche:*

    g) *Paper copy from microfiche:*

7. Method of payment

    a) *Loans:*   International Reply Coupons.

    b) *Photoduplicated material:*

8. *Loan period:* One month from date of receipt.

9. *Renewal:* No restrictions on renewals.

C. Narodna in univerzitetna Knjižnica, Ljubljana

2. b) *Despatch of loans:* Air mail, when requested.

    c) *Return of loans:* Air mail required from outside Europe.

3. b) *Despatch of photoduplicated material:* Air mail when requested.

4. *Restrictions:* Rare books, manuscripts, newspapers and periodicals are not lent; microfilms or photocopies of all these categories are available.

5. *Request forms accepted:* IFLA forms preferred.

6. Charges

    a) *Loans:* Postal charges may be waived by mutual agreement.

    b) *Photoduplicated material:*

    c) *35mm microfilm negative:*

    d) *35mm positive:*

    e) *Paper copy from microfilm:* } No information given.

    f) *Duplicate microfiche:*

    g) *Paper copy from microfiche:*

7. Method of payment

    a) *Loans:*

    b) *Photoduplicated material:* } International Reply Coupons.

8. *Loan period:* One month from date of receipt.

9. *Renewal:* A further month's renewal may be granted.

D. Centralna narodna biblioteka SR Crne Gore 'Djurdje Crnojević'

2. b) *Despatch of loans:* Registered surface mail.

    c) *Return of loans:* No information given.

3. b) *Despatch of photoduplicated material:* Registered surface mail.

4. *Restrictions:* Rare books, manuscripts and periodicals are not lent.

5. *Request forms accepted:* IFLA forms preferred.

6. Charges

    a) *Loans:* Postal costs.

    b) *Photoduplicated material:* 0,60 dinar per page.

    c) *35mm microfilm negative:*

    d) *35mm positive:*

    e) *Paper copy from microfilm:* } Not applicable.

    f) *Duplicate microfiche:*

    g) *Paper copy from microfiche:*

7. Method of payment

    a) *Loans:*

    b) *Photoduplicated material:* } International Reply Coupons.

8. *Loan period:* 20 days.

9. *Renewal:* Allowed.

E. Biblioteka Matice Srpske

In the Matica Srpske library interlending is carried out by the Circulation Department; there is no special lending collection. The library maintains the authority, subject and decimal number catalogues of monographs, the authority, decimal number and geographical catalogues of serials, and the central catalogue of Vojvodina. It cooperates with the central catalogue of Yugoslavia of the Yugoslav Bibliography Institute and participates in producing a database, the Union Catalog of the Yugoslav National Libraries.

2.   b)   *Despatch of loans:* Air mail.

     c)   *Return of loans:* Air mail not required.

3.   b)   *Despatch of photoduplicated material:* Air mail.

4.   *Restrictions:* Rare books, serials and books from the reference collection are not lent but microforms of the required publications may be supplied.

5.   *Request forms accepted:* IFLA forms.

6.   Charges

There is a reciprocal arrangement with some libraries, whereby no charges are made.

  a)   *Loans:* 12 DM. Lost items: 75 DM per book.

  b)   *Photoduplicated material:* 1,20 DM per page.

  c)   *35mm microfilm negative:* ⎫

                                       ⎬ 2,50 DM.

  d)   *35mm positive:* ⎭

  e)   *Paper copy from microfilm:* 4,50 DM per page (A4).

  f)   *Duplicate microfiche:* 2,50 DM.

  g)   *Paper copy from microfiche:* 4,50 DM per page (A4).

7.   Method of payment

  a)   *Loans:* ⎫

                                   ⎬ No information given.

  b)   *Photoduplicated material:* ⎭

8.   *Loan period:* 30 days.

9.   *Renewal:* Allowed for a further 30 days.

ZAMBIA*

1.   The system is based on the Zambia Library Service.

2.   a)   Requests for loans should be sent to:

     Zambia Library Service
     P.O Box 802
     Lusaka

  b)   *Despatch of loans:* Air mail.

  c)   *Return of loans:* Air mail.

3. a) Requests for photoduplicated material should be sent to:

    Address as in 2a above.

    b) *Despatch of photoduplicated material:* Air mail.

4. *Restrictions:* Reference books and journals are not lent; photocopies can be supplied on request.

5. *Request forms accepted:* Any.

6. Charges

    a) *Loans:* Free.

    b) *Photoduplicated material:* Up to 10 pages free. No further information given.

    c) *35mm microfilm negative:*

    d) *35mm positive:*

    e) *Paper copy from microfilm:* } No information given.

    f) *Duplicate microfiche:*

    g) *Paper copy from microfiche:*

7. Method of payment

    a) *Loans:* Not applicable.

    b) *Photoduplicated material:* Invoices are sent for photocopies over 10 pages.

8. *Loan period:* 2 months.

9. *Renewal:* Renewals of a further two months granted.

ZIMBABWE

1. The system is decentralised on the basis of COM Southern African Union Catalogues of monographs and periodicals, compiled and published by the State Library of South Africa. Libraries that do not subscribe to the Union Catalogues channel requests through the National Free Library.

2. a) Requests for loans should be sent to:

    National Free Library of Zimbabwe
    P.O Box 1773
    Bulawayo   **Telephone: 62359/69827**
                                          Telex: 33128 ZW

    b) *Despatch of loans:* Southern Africa: surface mail.
                            Elsewhere: air mail.

    c) *Return of loans:* Air mail is required from outside South Africa

3. a) Requests for photoduplicated material should be sent to:

    Address as in 2a above plus:

    National Archives of Zimbabwe
    P. Bag 7729
    Causeway
    Harare   **Telephone: 792741**

    b) *Despatch of photoduplicated material:* Air mail.

4. *Restrictions:* None of significance.

5. *Request forms accepted:* IFLA forms preferred for requests from outside Southern Africa.

6. Charges
   a) *Loans:* Postage costs for loans outside Southern Africa are recovered.
   b) *Photoduplicated material:* 30 cents per page.
   c) *35mm microfilm negative:* Z$ 90.00 per 31m.
   d) *35mm positive:* Z$ 45.00 per 31m (made from existing negative).
   e) *Paper copy from microfilm:*
   f) *Duplicate microfiche:* } Not applicable.
   g) *Paper copy from microfiche:*

7. Method of payment
   a) *Loans:* International Reply Coupons or bank draft.
   b) *Photoduplicated material:* Payable in advance by bank draft, cheque or postal order.

8. *Loan period:* 2 months.

9. *Renewal:* Renewals of one month at a time are granted.

10. *Additional information:*

    Outside Southern Africa loan material is normally supplied through the National Free Library and should be returned through the same library (with the exception of Inter-University Library Loans).